IPHONE 16
FOR SENIORS
AND BEGINNERS YOUR STRESS-
FREE IPHONE 16 GUIDE

Simplified, Illustrated, and Packed with Tips to Connect, Customize, and Feel Confident Every Day — Zero Tech Overload

JONAS TURING

TABLE OF CONTENTS

INTRODUCTION 5
Welcome & Purpose of the Guide 5
Overview of iPhone 16 Features & iOS 18 7
Transitioning from Other Devices (like Android) 11

CHAPTER 1
GETTING STARTED 15
Unboxing and Familiarizing with iPhone Components 15
Initial Setup: Apple ID, iCloud, and Wi-Fi 18
Essential Settings for New Users 21

CHAPTER 2
BASIC NAVIGATION 27
Home Screen and Lock Screen Overview 27
Using Touch Gestures, Action Button, and Voice Commands 31
Basics of Calling, Voicemail, and Contacts 34

CHAPTER 3
CUSTOMIZATION 38
Adjusting Display Brightness, Text Size, and Sound 38
Personalizing Ringtones, Wallpapers, and Widgets 43
Accessibility Options for Comfort and Ease 46

CHAPTER 4
BUILT-IN APPS FOR DAILY LIFE 51
Camera Basics: Taking and Viewing Photos 51
Essential Apps: Notes, Calendar, and Clock 55
Setting Up Reminders and Tasks 58

CHAPTER 5
STAYING CONNECTED 65
Sending Texts, Photos, and Video Messages 65
Basics of Social Media (Facebook, Messenger) 70
Email Setup and Management 75

CHAPTER 6
ONLINE SAFETY 81
Safe Browsing with Safari 81
Recognizing Scams and Avoiding Spam 87
Managing Privacy and App Permissions 93

CHAPTER 7

ADVANCED COMMUNICATION TOOLS 99
FaceTime for Video Calling 99
Group Messaging and Multimedia Sharing 105
Emergency SOS and Setting Up Medical ID 110

CHAPTER 8

DOWNLOADING AND MANAGING APPS 116
Navigating the App Store and Downloading Apps 116
Organizing, Deleting, and Updating Apps 121
Recommended Apps for Seniors (Health, Hobbies, Entertainment) ... 126
Tips for Finding and Using Apps 129

CHAPTER 9

PHOTOS & VIDEOS 130
Camera Tips and Photography Basics 130
Editing Photos and Videos on Your iPhone 136
Creating Albums and Sharing with Family 141

CHAPTER 10

APPLE PAY & WALLET 147
Setting Up Apple Pay and Digital Wallet 147
Making Payments Securely 152
Tips for Managing Payment Information 157

CHAPTER 11

HEALTH & FITNESS 164
Using the Health App for Activity Tracking 164
Setting Up Medical ID and Emergency Contacts 169
Exploring Mindfulness and Sleep Tracking 174

CHAPTER 12

TROUBLESHOOTING AND MAINTENANCE 181
Common Fixes for Wi-Fi, Bluetooth, and Apps 181
Managing Battery Life and Storage 186
Backing Up and Restoring Data with iCloud 191

CONCLUSION 197
Your Path to a Personalized Experience 197

GET YOUR EXCLUSIVE BONUS 200

INTRODUCTION

Welcome to iPhone 16 for Seniors and Beginners: Your Stress-Free iPhone 16 Guide! This introduction is here to help you feel at ease with your new device and ready to explore the wonderful tools it offers for connection, convenience, and personal enjoyment. This guide is designed to support you step-by-step, focusing on simplicity and confidence so that you can use your iPhone comfortably and independently. Even if you're new to smartphones or upgrading from an older model, this guide is structured to make your experience enjoyable and accessible, with every feature clearly explained and visually supported by screenshots and step-by-step instructions.

You might be wondering, "Why do I need this guide?" Many seniors and tech beginners feel a little overwhelmed by smartphones at first, and that's completely normal. Technology moves fast, but you don't have to feel rushed to catch up. This guide is here to make sure you never feel lost, with a pace that suits you, clear language that avoids confusing tech jargon, and practical tips that make daily tasks easier. Think of it as a friendly, patient companion for learning everything from setting up and personalizing your phone to using it safely for everyday tasks.

In this introductory chapter, we'll start with a warm welcome and a look at the purpose of this guide, so you know what to expect and how best to use it. We'll explore some of the exciting new features of the iPhone 16 and iOS 18, highlighting improvements designed to make using the phone more intuitive and enjoyable, whether you're texting with family, organizing reminders, or even tracking your health. Finally, we'll cover some helpful tips for those transitioning from other devices, like Android phones, so you can smoothly adjust to the iPhone's unique features and layout.

Using a smartphone can be a great way to connect with family, discover new interests, and make daily tasks simpler. And it doesn't have to be stressful. With this guide, you're in control of the learning process. Each chapter builds on the last, covering everything from basic functions and essential apps to customization options and online safety. Throughout, you'll find reassuring language, tips to keep your information safe, and practical suggestions for personalizing your iPhone to fit your preferences and needs.

So take a deep breath and remember that you're in good hands. You're about to embark on a journey to master the iPhone 16, and you're already on the right track by starting here. This introduction is your first step toward becoming comfortable and confident with your new device. Don't feel rushed—take your time, enjoy the learning process, and know that you can always revisit any section if you need a refresher. Your iPhone is more than just a phone; it's a tool for connection, creativity, and convenience, and this guide is here to help you make the most of it, every step of the way.

Welcome & Purpose of the Guide

Welcome to iPhone 16 for Seniors and Beginners: Your Stress-Free iPhone 16 Guide! This guide is designed to be a reliable companion, offering step-by-step instructions, clear visuals, and practical examples tailored to help seniors and beginners make the most of the iPhone 16. If you're new to smartphones or upgrading from an older model, this book is crafted to walk you through everything from setup to more advanced features, without the stress of overly technical language or complicated steps. It's normal to feel a bit overwhelmed with new technology, but this guide is here to make the learning process enjoyable and approachable.

Whether you received your iPhone 16 as a gift or decided to purchase it to stay connected with family and friends, you've made a wonderful choice. The iPhone 16 is a user-friendly device with various features that are helpful, fun, and empowering. The key to feeling confident with your new phone lies in understanding the basics first, then gradually exploring more advanced functions as you become comfortable. That's why this guide is structured to start with the essentials, building your knowledge in small, manageable steps.

The purpose of this guide is to simplify your experience with the iPhone 16. You'll learn how to set up your phone, personalize it to suit your needs, and use it to connect with loved ones and stay organized. Each section in the guide has been thoughtfully designed to break down key tasks, such as making calls, sending texts, or setting reminders, into easy-to-follow steps with plenty of visuals to support your understanding. With clear screenshots and instructions, you'll be able to see exactly what each feature looks like on your screen, helping you feel more comfortable and confident as you learn.

One of the primary reasons many seniors and beginners seek guidance on using smartphones is because technology can often seem complicated and intimidating. The iPhone, with its sleek design and ever-evolving features, may feel overwhelming at first. However, Apple has put a lot of thought into making its devices as user-friendly as possible, and this guide builds on that by removing technical jargon, explaining features in plain language, and focusing on everyday tasks. Think of this guide as a friendly teacher who is here to make each task accessible, whether it's as simple as setting an alarm or as exciting as learning to FaceTime with family across the country.

This guide also values the importance of independence. Many people want to be able to use their devices without relying on others for constant help. Mastering your iPhone will give you the ability to explore apps, customize your settings, and handle everyday tasks independently. And independence doesn't mean rushing through the material; instead, it's about taking things one step at a time, focusing on small wins, and building a foundation that allows you to gradually take on more. As you move through each chapter, you'll gain a sense of accomplishment, knowing that you're developing a skill set that will make your life more connected and convenient.

Another core purpose of this guide is to foster a sense of connection. Many iPhone features are specifically designed to help you stay close to your loved ones, whether they live next door or across the world. The iPhone 16 makes it easy to share photos, chat over video, and connect through messages. This guide will show you how to use these tools so you can feel part of your children's and grandchildren's lives, sharing in their experiences and staying updated with ease. Knowing how to use FaceTime, for example, allows you to have face-to-face conversations, making distance feel a little smaller. Understanding how to send and receive pictures enables you to celebrate family milestones and relive happy memories. These features not only make communication easier, but they also help create lasting bonds and memories.

One of the special elements of this guide is the interactive "Practice What You've Learned" section at the end of each chapter. These sections provide simple exercises and quizzes designed to reinforce what you've read, ensuring that you feel confident before moving on to the next topic. These exercises are meant to be enjoyable, giving you a chance to apply what you've learned and providing gentle reminders of key concepts. Don't worry if you don't get everything right the first time—these are opportunities for practice, not tests. They're included so you can take each lesson at your own pace and feel comfortable revisiting any part of the guide whenever you need a refresher.

While this guide aims to build confidence and familiarity with the iPhone, it's also structured to emphasize safety. In today's digital world, security is a top concern for many. This book covers essential privacy and security tips to keep your information safe, such as setting up a secure passcode, recognizing potential scams, and understanding how to manage app permissions. These sections are written with simplicity in mind, avoiding unnecessary complexity while giving you the information you need to use your iPhone with peace of mind.

Alongside safety, customization is another focus of this guide. The iPhone 16 has a range of settings designed to adapt to individual needs and preferences. You can adjust text size for easier reading, set up hearing aid compatibility, and customize notifications so you only receive alerts that matter to you. This guide will walk you through the different customization options, so you can make your iPhone a device that feels uniquely yours. Personalizing your iPhone is a wonderful way to create a comfortable, enjoyable experience that reflects your own needs and lifestyle.

One of the most enjoyable aspects of using the iPhone is discovering all the little things it can do to make life easier. From using the calendar to keep track of appointments to setting reminders for medication, the iPhone 16 is packed with features that help with daily organization. This guide covers a range of practical tools and apps, focusing on real-life scenarios that are relevant to seniors and beginners. You'll also explore features like the Health app, which can track steps, monitor heart rate, and even offer reminders for health check-ins, making it a valuable tool for wellness.

To sum up, the purpose of this guide is to empower you with knowledge, independence, and confidence in using your iPhone 16. With each chapter, you'll build a new layer of understanding, helping you feel more comfortable navigating your device. By the end of this book, our goal is for you to see the iPhone not just as a piece of technology, but as a valuable companion that enhances your daily life, keeps you connected with loved ones, and gives you the tools to stay organized and engaged with the world.

So take a deep breath, open your iPhone 16, and let's get started. Remember, you're in control of the pace and process. This guide is here to make your journey smooth, enjoyable, and entirely stress-free. Welcome aboard!

Overview of iPhone 16 Features & iOS 18

The iPhone 16 introduces a range of innovative features that enhance usability, security, and personalization, making it one of Apple's most user-friendly models yet. Paired with the latest iOS 18 software, this device is designed to offer a seamless experience for both beginners and seasoned iPhone users. Whether you're interested in connecting with loved ones, organizing your day-to-day tasks, or exploring new hobbies, the iPhone 16 provides tools to do so in a straightforward and enjoyable way. This overview highlights the key features of the iPhone 16 and iOS 18, giving you a taste of the powerful functions available right at your fingertips.

Remove a control.

Resize a control.

Open the controls gallery.

One of the standout features of the iPhone 16 is its improved display. The high-resolution, bright screen makes it easy to read text and view images with incredible clarity. This enhancement is especially beneficial for users who may struggle with smaller text or need sharper visuals. Additionally, iOS 18 offers a variety of customization options to tailor the display to your needs. For example, you can increase the text size and adjust the brightness with just a few taps, making reading messages or browsing the web more comfortable. The new "Always-On" display option allows you to keep important information visible even when the phone is locked, so you can quickly glance at the time, weather, or calendar without unlocking your device.

The Home Screen also offers more customization than ever. With the addition of interactive widgets, you can personalize your screen to display essential information, such as the latest news, your health stats, or recent photos of loved ones. Widgets are like mini-apps that show you quick information at a glance, and you can arrange them however you like on your screen. This makes the iPhone 16 a highly adaptable device, capable of catering to individual preferences and needs.

For those who love capturing memories, the iPhone 16's camera capabilities are a game-changer. The camera system now features improved low-light performance, so you can take clear photos even in dim lighting. Night Mode, which was already popular on previous iPhone models, has been enhanced to produce even better images, making it ideal for snapping photos of family gatherings or evening outings. Portrait Mode, which blurs the background to emphasize the subject, now has more customization options, allowing you to create professional-quality photos with ease.

The iPhone 16 also includes a new feature called "Photographic Styles," which allows you to adjust the look of your photos in real-time. This feature lets you choose from different styles, such as "Rich Contrast" or "Vibrant," which automatically adjust colors and tones to give each picture a unique feel. If you enjoy photography, these features make it easy to add a creative touch to your photos without needing any technical knowledge. Additionally, the enhanced zoom options let you capture detailed shots from a distance, whether it's a beautiful landscape or a family event.

iOS 18 continues Apple's commitment to making its devices accessible to everyone. The new features in iOS 18 are designed with a focus on inclusivity, making it easier for individuals with visual, hearing, or mobility challenges to use the iPhone independently. For instance, the "Voice Control" feature allows you to navigate your iPhone using only your voice, making it possible to perform tasks hands-free. This can be particularly useful for answering calls, composing messages, or even adjusting settings without having to touch the screen.

Another useful feature is "Magnifier," which transforms the iPhone's camera into a powerful digital magnifying glass, allowing users to zoom in on fine print or distant objects. Additionally, the iPhone 16 is compatible with a wide range of hearing aids, providing seamless audio streaming and adjustments that make conversations and media playback clearer. Accessibility options are easily adjustable in the iPhone's settings, so you can personalize them to match your needs.

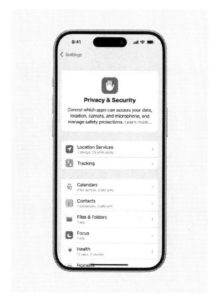

With the increased focus on privacy in today's digital world, the iPhone 16 and iOS 18 offer a suite of security features to keep your data safe. Face ID, Apple's facial recognition technology, has been enhanced for faster and more secure unlocking, allowing you to access your device quickly while ensuring only you can do so. iOS 18 also includes a privacy dashboard that gives you an overview of which apps have access to sensitive information, such as your location or contacts. This dashboard makes it easy to manage app permissions and helps you maintain control over your personal data.

One of the newest privacy features is "App Privacy Reports," which shows you how frequently apps access your information. This transparency empowers you to make informed decisions about which apps to trust. Furthermore, Apple has introduced "Mail Privacy Protection," which prevents senders from knowing when you open an email or tracking your location through your IP address. These added privacy options allow you to use your iPhone confidently, knowing that your personal information is safeguarded.

The iPhone 16, paired with iOS 18, offers an expanded suite of health and wellness tools. The Health app now includes even more tracking options for wellness activities, allowing you to monitor steps, track sleep, and even log your mental wellness through mood tracking. You can set reminders for medication, monitor your heart rate, and view an overview of your health metrics, which can be shared with healthcare providers if desired. The integration of health data is easy to use and beneficial for anyone interested in staying proactive about their health.

Another important feature is the "Medical ID," which stores critical health information such as allergies, medical conditions, and emergency contacts. Medical ID can be accessed from the lock screen, enabling first responders to quickly access necessary information in an emergency. Combined with the "Emergency SOS" feature, which allows you to contact emergency services by pressing the side button, these features make the iPhone 16 a valuable tool for health and safety.

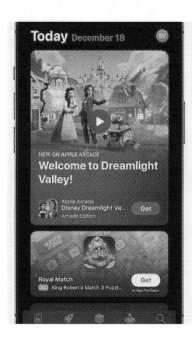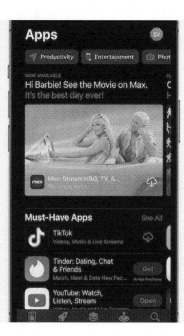

The App Store in iOS 18 has been updated to make it easier to discover apps suited to your needs. A new "For You" section curates app recommendations based on your usage, helping you find tools that may be of interest, whether for hobbies, health, or entertainment. Additionally, the App Library feature organizes all your apps into categories, so you can quickly locate any app without cluttering your home screen. This is especially helpful for keeping your apps organized and easy to access.

The App Store also highlights a wide range of apps for seniors, such as health tracking, memory games, or social media apps to connect with family and friends. iOS 18 ensures that each app is vetted for quality and safety, so you can download new apps confidently.

The iPhone 16 is designed to work seamlessly with other Apple devices, such as iPads, Apple Watches, and Mac computers. Through iCloud, all your photos, contacts, and files are securely stored and can be accessed across devices. This means you can take a photo on your iPhone and view it on your iPad without any extra steps. FaceTime, Apple's video calling service, now supports group calls with up to 32 participants, making it easy to connect with multiple friends or family members at once.

In iOS 18, FaceTime also includes new features like spatial audio and grid view, which create a more natural, immersive video calling experience. You can now even share your screen with others on FaceTime, making it easy to show a family member how to use a feature or share a photo album.

Transitioning from Other Devices (like Android)

Switching to a new phone can feel intimidating, especially when moving from one operating system to another, such as Android to iOS on the iPhone 16. Fortunately, Apple has designed its devices with ease of use in mind, making the transition smoother than you might expect. This section will guide you through the differences between Android and iOS, help you understand key features on your iPhone, and show you how to transfer your important data and apps. By the end of this section, you'll feel confident navigating your new device and ready to enjoy all the benefits the iPhone 16 has to offer.

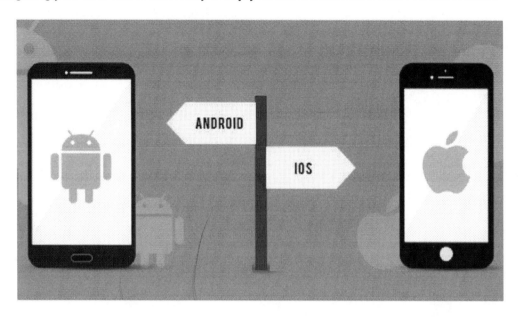

The first step in a smooth transition is understanding some of the main differences in how Android and iOS devices are structured. While both systems allow you to perform similar tasks—such as making calls, sending messages, browsing the web, and downloading apps—the layout and processes can vary significantly.

- **Home Screen Organization**: Unlike many Android phones, which have both a home screen and an app drawer, the iPhone's home screen displays all installed apps by default. If you prefer a clutter-free look, iOS 18 introduces the App Library, which automatically organizes your apps into categories and allows you to hide specific apps from the main home screen. To access it, simply swipe to the right-most screen.
- **Control Center**: On Android, quick settings are typically accessed by swiping down from the top of the screen. On the iPhone, you can access similar functions—like Wi-Fi, Bluetooth, and brightness—through the Control Center, which you open by swiping down from the top-right corner. The Control Center is highly customizable, allowing you to add or remove shortcuts for settings you use most often.
- **Navigation Gestures**: Android devices often use a combination of back, home, and recent apps buttons for navigation. The iPhone, however, relies on gesture-based navigation. Swiping up from the bottom of the screen returns you to the home screen, while swiping up and holding brings up recent apps. To go back, you can swipe from the left edge of the screen. These gestures may take some getting used to, but with a bit of practice, they can feel quite intuitive.

Apple has simplified the setup process for new iPhone users, especially those transitioning from Android. When you turn on your iPhone for the first time, you'll be guided through an easy setup process that helps you connect to Wi-Fi, create an Apple ID, and customize essential settings.

- **Apple ID**: The Apple ID is similar to a Google account on Android—it serves as your personal account for all Apple services, including the App Store, iCloud, and iMessage. If you don't already have an Apple ID, you'll be prompted to create one during setup. It's important to remember your Apple ID login information, as you'll use it frequently for downloading apps and accessing your data across Apple devices.
- **Transferring Data from Android**: Apple has developed an app called "Move to iOS," which simplifies the process of transferring data from an Android device to an iPhone. Download the Move to iOS app on your Android phone, follow the on-screen instructions, and it will transfer contacts, message history, photos, videos, web bookmarks, and more to your iPhone. This app ensures that your important data moves with you, reducing the need to manually reconfigure everything.
- **iCloud and Syncing**: While Android primarily uses Google services for cloud storage and syncing, Apple relies on iCloud. During setup, you'll have the option to enable iCloud, which allows you to back up photos, contacts, calendars, and documents and access them on any Apple device. You can also use iCloud Drive to store files that can be accessed from any internet-connected device.

One of the most noticeable differences between Android and iOS is the App Store, which is the exclusive source for downloading apps on iPhones. Apple carefully vets each app for quality and security, ensuring that the App Store is a safe environment for downloading software. If you were using Google services on your Android device, don't worry—you can still access many Google apps, such as Gmail, Google Photos, and Google Maps, on your iPhone through the App Store.

- **Messaging and Communication**: On Android, SMS messages and calls are often managed through apps like Google Messages. On the iPhone, Apple provides iMessage for messaging and FaceTime for video and audio calls. iMessage is a secure messaging service that allows you to send texts, photos, and videos to other Apple users over Wi-Fi or cellular data without using SMS. FaceTime, which is pre-installed, offers high-quality video and audio calls, making it easy to stay connected with friends and family who also use Apple devices.
- **App Ecosystem and iCloud Integration**: iOS apps are deeply integrated with iCloud, which allows you to sync your data across devices. For example, if you take a photo on your iPhone, it's automatically saved to iCloud Photos and accessible on your iPad or Mac. Similarly, if you save notes or reminders, they sync seamlessly across all Apple devices. This integration makes it easy to switch between devices without missing a beat, a feature that may be new if you're coming from Android.
- **Siri and Voice Commands**: The iPhone's voice assistant, Siri, is similar to Google Assistant on Android. Siri can help with a variety of tasks, from setting reminders and sending messages to answering questions and playing music. You can activate Siri by saying "Hey Siri" or by pressing and holding the side button. Siri is highly customizable, and you can adjust its settings to best suit your needs.

Personalization is an important part of making a new device feel like your own, and iOS 18 offers a variety of settings to tailor your iPhone 16 to your liking. Some customization options may be familiar from your Android experience, but others may be new and worth exploring.

- **Display and Accessibility Settings**: iOS 18 allows you to customize the display to make it easier to read and use. You can increase the text size, adjust brightness, and even switch to Dark Mode for a softer display in low light. Additionally, Apple's extensive accessibility options let you enable features like Voice Control, Magnifier, and hearing aid compatibility, ensuring that your device is comfortable to use, regardless of any physical limitations.
- **Ringtones and Notification Settings**: Changing your ringtone or notification sound is straightforward on an iPhone. Apple offers a selection of tones, or you can purchase custom tones from the iTunes Store. Notifications are also highly customizable, and you can control which apps send you alerts and how they appear. For example, you can allow calls to show up as banners or pop-ups, and you can set message notifications to appear on the lock screen, ensuring you don't miss important alerts.
- **Widgets and the App Library**: iOS 18 introduces interactive widgets that you can add to your home screen for quick access to essential information, such as weather, news, or calendar events. Widgets can be resized and rearranged to fit your needs, adding an extra layer of convenience. The App Library organizes all your apps in one place, making it easy to locate what you need without cluttering your main screens.

Switching from Android to iPhone is a significant change, and it's okay to take your time adjusting to the new interface. Here are some tips to help you feel more comfortable:

- **Practice Makes Perfect**: Familiarizing yourself with new gestures and the layout of iOS may feel odd at first, but with practice, it will become second nature. Try exploring different parts of the Control Center and settings to see what options are available and what feels most comfortable for you.

- **Use Apple Support and Tutorials**: Apple offers extensive support resources, including tutorials and guided sessions at Apple Stores, if you have one nearby. The built-in "Tips" app on your iPhone also provides quick tips and tutorials to help you discover new features and shortcuts.

- **Stay Organized with Folders and the App Library**: If you had a specific way of organizing your apps on Android, try replicating it on your iPhone. Use folders to keep similar apps together and take advantage of the App Library to reduce clutter on your home screen.

Transitioning to an iPhone from an Android device is a learning experience, but with patience, you'll find it can be both rewarding and enjoyable. This guide will support you along the way, and before you know it, your iPhone 16 will feel like second nature. Enjoy the journey, and remember, this new device is here to make your life easier, more connected, and more fun!

CHAPTER 1
GETTING STARTED

Welcome to Chapter 1! This chapter is all about getting comfortable with your new iPhone 16 from the very beginning. If you've just unboxed your iPhone and are ready to dive in, this chapter will guide you through the essential steps to set up your device, connect it to the internet, and adjust important settings to suit your needs. For anyone feeling uncertain about where to start, don't worry—you're in the right place, and each step is designed to be simple, straightforward, and beginner-friendly.

Starting with the basics, this chapter will begin by introducing the physical components of your iPhone. Knowing what each button, port, and feature does will make it easier to navigate your device and understand its functionality. From the action button to the volume controls, we'll go over each part of your iPhone to ensure you're familiar with everything at your fingertips. This way, when you're learning new tasks, you'll already feel at ease with the device itself.

Next, we'll guide you through the initial setup of your iPhone, focusing on creating an Apple ID, setting up iCloud, and connecting to Wi-Fi. Your Apple ID is your personal account with Apple, allowing you to access essential services like the App Store, iMessage, and FaceTime. Creating an Apple ID is straightforward, and this section will break down each step so you can set it up smoothly. We'll also cover iCloud, which is Apple's cloud service that securely stores your data, such as photos and contacts, so you can access it from any Apple device. Setting up iCloud is especially helpful for data backup, giving you peace of mind that your information is safe.

Connecting to Wi-Fi is another key step covered in this chapter. With your iPhone connected to the internet, you can use apps, browse the web, and keep your device updated with the latest features. The chapter will walk you through finding available Wi-Fi networks and entering a password, if necessary. This process is similar to other devices, but if it's new to you, we'll make sure you're connected with ease.

Finally, this chapter will guide you through some essential settings to make your iPhone experience as comfortable and efficient as possible. These settings cover important basics, such as adjusting the display brightness, setting up security with Face ID or a passcode, and managing notifications so you're only alerted to the things that matter most. We'll also take a look at Accessibility settings, designed to make the iPhone easier to use for anyone with specific vision, hearing, or physical needs. Customizing these settings ensures that your iPhone is tailored to suit you, from text size to sound adjustments.

This chapter is your foundation, giving you the skills and confidence to start using your iPhone with ease. By the end of it, you'll have a fully set up iPhone, configured to match your preferences and ready for exploring more advanced features. Let's get started and make sure your first steps with the iPhone 16 are simple, smooth, and enjoyable!

Unboxing and Familiarizing with iPhone Components

Getting a new iPhone is exciting, and unboxing it for the first time is the perfect opportunity to get acquainted with its physical features and components. This section will guide you through the unboxing process, showing you what comes in the box and helping you understand the main components of your new iPhone 16. Knowing each part of your device will make it easier to follow along as you explore new functions and features. So let's start by unpacking everything and identifying each part of the iPhone 16.

As you open the box, you'll first see your iPhone 16 resting on top. Apple's packaging is carefully designed to protect your device and present it beautifully, and each item included in the box has a purpose. Here's what you'll find:

- **The iPhone 16**: This is, of course, the main item. Gently lift it out of the box, and you'll notice that it's covered with a protective film to prevent any scratches or smudges during packaging. You can remove this film by peeling it off from one corner.
- **USB-C to Lightning Cable**: Apple has included a USB-C to Lightning cable for charging and data transfer. One end of the cable has a USB-C connector, which you'll plug into a power adapter or a compatible USB-C port on your computer. The other end is the Lightning connector, which fits into your iPhone's charging port.
- **SIM Card Ejector Tool**: You'll also find a small metal pin, which is the SIM card ejector tool. This tool is used to open the SIM card tray, where you can insert or remove your SIM card to connect to your cellular network.
- **Quick Start Guide and Stickers**: In a small envelope, you'll find a quick start guide, warranty information, and Apple's signature stickers. The quick start guide provides a few basic setup steps, while the stickers are a fun way to show your Apple pride.
- **Power Adapter**: Note that Apple no longer includes a power adapter in the box with the iPhone. If you don't already have a USB-C power adapter, you may need to purchase one separately to charge your iPhone. Any USB-C power adapter should work, but using an Apple-certified adapter is recommended for the best performance.

Now that you have your iPhone 16 in hand, let's explore each of its key components. Familiarizing yourself with these parts will help you understand how the device operates and where to access various features.

- **The Display**: The front of your iPhone is dominated by its beautiful, high-resolution display. This screen is where you'll interact with apps, view photos, make video calls, and more. With an "edge-to-edge" design, the display extends almost to the edges of the phone, giving you a larger screen area for an immersive experience. The iPhone 16's display is bright and sharp, making it easy to read text and view images clearly.

- **The Front Camera and Face ID Sensors**: At the top of the screen, you'll see a small notch or cutout, which houses the front camera and Face ID sensors. Face ID is Apple's facial recognition technology that securely unlocks your iPhone by recognizing your face. This feature is convenient and secure, allowing you to unlock your device, make payments, and access apps without needing to enter a passcode.
- **Volume Buttons**: On the left side of your iPhone, you'll find the volume buttons, which are used to adjust the sound level on your device. Press the top button to increase the volume and the bottom button to decrease it. You'll use these buttons frequently, not only for calls and media but also for adjusting sound levels in apps and games.
- **The Action Button (formerly Mute Switch)**: Also located on the left side, just above the volume buttons, is the Action button. This button used to be the mute switch on previous iPhone models, but now it's customizable to perform different actions, like quickly muting your phone, launching the camera, activating Do Not Disturb, or opening a specific app. You can configure the Action button to suit your preferences, making it a handy shortcut for commonly used features.
- **The Power/Side Button**: The power button, located on the right side of your iPhone, has multiple functions. Press it once to lock or wake up the screen, or press and hold it to activate Siri, Apple's voice assistant. The power button is also used to turn your device off—simply press and hold it along with one of the volume buttons to bring up the option to power down. When your iPhone is powered off, holding this button will turn it back on.
- **The SIM Card Tray**: On the right side, just below the power button, you'll find the SIM card tray. If you're using a physical SIM card from your cellular provider, you'll insert it here. To open the SIM tray, use the ejector tool provided in the box. Insert the tool into the small hole on the tray, press gently, and the tray will pop out for you to insert your SIM card.
- **The Lightning Port**: At the bottom of your iPhone, you'll see the Lightning port, which is used for charging and data transfer. Plug the Lightning connector end of your cable into this port, and connect the other end to a power adapter or computer to charge your device. The Lightning port can also connect accessories, like headphones with a Lightning connector, although Apple has transitioned away from including headphones in the box.
- **Speakers and Microphone**: The speakers and microphone are also located at the bottom of your iPhone, flanking the Lightning port. The speakers provide high-quality audio for phone calls, music, videos, and more. The microphone picks up your voice for calls and voice commands, and it's designed to reduce background noise for clearer audio quality.

Before you begin using your iPhone, consider applying a screen protector and using a case to protect it from accidental bumps or drops. The iPhone's glass and aluminum design is durable, but extra protection can help keep it in pristine condition for years to come.

- **Screen Protector**: Screen protectors are available in various materials, with tempered glass being a popular choice for durability. Applying a screen protector can prevent scratches and minimize fingerprints on your display.
- **Case Options**: Cases come in many styles, from clear cases that show off your iPhone's design to protective cases that offer shock absorption. Find a case that matches your style and comfort level; many also include extra grip to make the device easier to hold.

Now that you're familiar with the parts of your iPhone 16, you're ready to proceed with the initial setup, where you'll create an Apple ID, set up iCloud, and connect to Wi-Fi. Getting acquainted with each component will make future steps easier, and knowing your device's layout will help you navigate it comfortably. With this foundational knowledge, you're prepared to move forward confidently in setting up your iPhone to suit your preferences and needs. Enjoy your new device—it's designed to make life easier, more connected, and even a bit more fun!

Initial Setup: Apple ID, iCloud, and Wi-Fi

Setting up a new iPhone is an exciting experience, and Apple has streamlined the initial setup process to be straightforward and user-friendly. This section will walk you through creating an Apple ID, setting up iCloud for secure storage, and connecting to Wi-Fi, which are essential first steps to getting the most out of your iPhone 16. These initial steps will not only personalize your device but also provide access to Apple's wide range of services, ensuring your data is backed up and that you're connected to the internet. Let's dive into each setup step to make sure your iPhone is ready to go.

Your Apple ID is a personal account that gives you access to Apple's ecosystem of apps, services, and features. It's similar to a Google account for Android users, acting as a unique identifier that allows you to download apps from the App Store, back up data to iCloud, and use features like iMessage and FaceTime. If you don't already have an Apple ID, creating one during the initial setup is essential. Here's how to set it up:

- **Step 1**: When you turn on your iPhone for the first time, you'll see a "Hello" screen. Follow the on-screen instructions to choose your language and region.
- **Step 2**: After setting up a few basic preferences, you'll be prompted to sign in with your Apple ID. If you have one already, simply enter your email address and password. If you don't, tap on "Create a new Apple ID."
- **Step 3**: You'll need to enter a few details, such as your name, date of birth, and a preferred email address. This email will be used as your Apple ID username, so choose an address that you check frequently.
- **Step 4**: Create a strong password for your Apple ID. Apple requires a combination of uppercase letters, lowercase letters, and numbers to ensure security. Remember this password, as you'll need it whenever you download apps, make purchases, or access certain settings.
- **Step 5**: Set up two-factor authentication. This adds an extra layer of security by requiring a verification code sent to a trusted device or phone number whenever you sign in from a new device.

Once your Apple ID is set up, you'll be able to access Apple's services, including iCloud, the App Store, and iTunes. Your Apple ID is the gateway to your iPhone's full capabilities, so take a moment to write down your password or save it in a secure location.

iCloud is Apple's cloud storage service, designed to keep your data—like photos, contacts, calendars, and documents—safely backed up and accessible across all your Apple devices. Setting up iCloud ensures that your information is protected and that you can retrieve your data if you ever lose or upgrade your device. Here's how to set up and customize iCloud:

- **Step 1**: During the setup process, after creating your Apple ID, you'll be prompted to set up iCloud. You can choose which iCloud services you want to enable, such as Photos, Contacts, Calendars, and Backup.
- **Step 2**: If you'd like to store photos in iCloud, enabling **iCloud Photos** will automatically upload and store your photos and videos, allowing you to access them from any Apple device. iCloud Photos is especially useful if you take a lot of pictures and want to ensure they're safe and accessible.
- **Step 3**: Enable **iCloud Backup** to automatically back up your iPhone's data, such as app data, device settings, messages, and more. This way, if you ever need to restore your iPhone or upgrade to a new one, you can easily transfer all your information.
- **Step 4**: Choose whether you want to enable **Find My iPhone**, which is a security feature that helps you locate your device if it's lost or stolen. You can track your iPhone's location using the Find My app on another device or through iCloud.com, making it a valuable tool for security and peace of mind.

iCloud offers 5 GB of free storage, which should cover basic backups and documents. However, if you plan on storing a large number of photos, videos, or apps, you may want to consider upgrading to a larger storage plan. Apple offers affordable monthly plans, which you can select through your iCloud settings.

A Wi-Fi connection is essential for fully utilizing your iPhone's capabilities, allowing you to browse the internet, use apps, and download content without using cellular data. Connecting to Wi-Fi during the initial setup also ensures that your iPhone can update software, download apps, and sync with iCloud. Here's how to connect to Wi-Fi:

- **Step 1**: During setup, you'll see a screen prompting you to connect to a Wi-Fi network. Your iPhone will automatically search for available networks and display a list.
- **Step 2**: Find your Wi-Fi network in the list and tap on it. You'll be asked to enter the network password. This is usually found on your internet router or provided by your internet service provider.
- **Step 3**: After entering the password, tap "Join" to connect to the network. Once connected, you'll see a checkmark next to the network name, indicating that you're online.

Connecting to Wi-Fi not only conserves your cellular data but also allows your iPhone to automatically back up to iCloud, update apps, and check for new software updates. If you're at home, your iPhone will remember your Wi-Fi network and reconnect automatically whenever you're in range.

In addition to Apple ID, iCloud, and Wi-Fi, there are a few more essential settings that Apple walks you through during the initial setup process to enhance your experience and keep your device secure:

- **Face ID or Passcode Setup**: For added security, Apple encourages users to set up Face ID, Apple's facial recognition system. Face ID uses the front-facing camera to scan and recognize your face, allowing you to unlock your iPhone with just a glance. If you prefer, you can set a passcode instead. Having Face ID or a passcode secures your device and protects your personal information from unauthorized access.
- **Location Services**: Location Services allows apps to use your location to provide relevant information, like nearby restaurants or traffic updates. You'll be asked if you want to enable Location Services during setup. You can choose to allow or restrict access to specific apps later in your Settings.
- **Siri and Voice Activation**: Siri is Apple's voice assistant, which can help with tasks like setting reminders, sending messages, and finding information online. During setup, you'll have the option to enable "Hey Siri," which allows you to activate Siri by saying, "Hey Siri." You can then ask questions or give commands without touching your iPhone.

Setting up a new iPhone can be exciting, but it can also involve several steps. Here are a few tips to ensure a smooth and stress-free setup:

- **Take Your Time**: Don't feel rushed. The setup process is designed to be straightforward, but if you're new to iPhones or unsure about any step, take a moment to read the on-screen instructions carefully.
- **Keep Your Wi-Fi Password Handy**: Having your Wi-Fi password ready will save you time. If you're unsure about your Wi-Fi details, you can often find them on your internet router or by contacting your internet provider.
- **Write Down Your Apple ID and Password**: Your Apple ID is an important account that you'll use frequently. Write down your Apple ID username and password in a secure place, such as a password manager or a physical notebook, so you can access it if you forget.

Once you've completed these steps, your iPhone 16 will be set up and ready to use! You'll now have a fully personalized device with access to Apple's services, secure backups through iCloud, and a reliable Wi-Fi connection. With these essentials in place, you can begin exploring all the wonderful features your iPhone has to offer. The setup process is a great first step toward making your iPhone an enjoyable, convenient, and secure part of your daily life.

Essential Settings for New Users

Now that your iPhone 16 is set up, it's time to explore and customize essential settings that will make your experience both comfortable and efficient. These initial adjustments will help you personalize the device according to your needs and ensure that you're getting the most out of the iPhone's features. We'll cover important settings for display and sound, security, notifications, and accessibility options—all designed to make your iPhone easy to use, whether you're new to smartphones or simply want a more customized experience.

One of the first settings you may want to adjust is your iPhone's display, which can be customized to suit your comfort level. Display settings control brightness, text size, and the appearance of the screen in different lighting conditions. Adjusting these will ensure that your screen is comfortable to look at, whether you're reading, browsing, or watching videos.

- **Brightness**: You can adjust the brightness level of your iPhone in **Settings > Display & Brightness**. A brighter screen is useful for outdoor environments, while a dimmer screen can be more comfortable in low-light conditions. Additionally, you can enable **Auto-Brightness**, which automatically adjusts brightness based on the surrounding light.
- **Text Size and Bold Text**: For better readability, you can increase the text size and make it bold. Go to **Settings > Display & Brightness > Text Size**, where you can use the slider to choose a larger font. In the same section, you'll see an option for **Bold Text**, which makes the font bolder, enhancing readability.
- **Dark Mode**: If you find it easier to look at a darker screen, you can enable Dark Mode in **Settings > Display & Brightness**. This feature changes the color scheme to dark colors, reducing glare, especially in low-light environments. You can set Dark Mode to automatically turn on at sunset or choose "Always On" if you prefer a darker screen throughout the day.

Your iPhone's sound settings allow you to control everything from ringtones to vibration feedback. Here's how to adjust sound options to suit your preferences:

- **Ringtones and Alerts**: To set a ringtone, go to **Settings > Sounds & Haptics**. You can choose from a selection of default ringtones or even purchase custom ringtones from the iTunes Store. In this section, you can also set alert tones for notifications, alarms, and messages.

- **Volume Control**: The **Sounds & Haptics** menu also lets you adjust the volume for your ringtone and alerts. If you want to be able to quickly adjust volume, you can use the physical volume buttons on the side of the iPhone.
- **Vibration and Haptic Feedback**: iPhones come with haptic feedback, which provides subtle vibrations to enhance the touch experience. You can enable or disable vibration feedback for incoming calls and alerts, or adjust how strongly you feel these haptics.

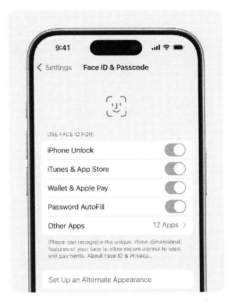

Keeping your iPhone secure is essential, and Face ID and passcode settings are two effective ways to protect your personal information. Here's how to set them up:

- **Face ID**: Face ID uses facial recognition to unlock your phone, make payments, and access secure apps. Go to **Settings > Face ID & Passcode** and follow the instructions to set up Face ID. Hold your iPhone at face level, and it will scan your face to create a secure map. This map is used exclusively on your device and provides a convenient, secure way to unlock your phone.
- **Passcode**: Even if you use Face ID, it's wise to set a passcode as a backup. In **Settings > Face ID & Passcode**, you can create a six-digit passcode or choose an alphanumeric code for added security. You'll be prompted to enter your passcode in situations where Face ID isn't available, such as after restarting your iPhone.

Notifications are alerts that let you know when you have new messages, app updates, reminders, and other important information. By adjusting notification settings, you can ensure that you're only notified about the things that matter most to you, avoiding unnecessary distractions.

- **Managing Notifications**: Go to **Settings > Notifications** to see a list of apps and customize notifications for each one. For instance, you can choose to receive banner notifications, sounds, or both. If you'd rather not see notifications on your lock screen, you can disable them for specific apps.
- **Scheduled Summary**: iOS 18 includes a feature called **Scheduled Summary**, which lets you receive notifications in batches at specific times instead of throughout the day. This can be useful if you want to avoid being constantly interrupted. Enable Scheduled Summary in the Notifications settings and select which apps you want to include in the summary.
- **Do Not Disturb**: In **Settings > Focus > Do Not Disturb**, you can activate Do Not Disturb mode, which silences all notifications and calls for a set period. This is ideal for uninterrupted work time or sleep. You can customize Do Not Disturb to allow calls from specific contacts, so you won't miss important calls from family members.

Privacy is a priority on the iPhone, and Apple provides several options to protect your personal information. Here's how to manage key privacy settings:

- **Location Services**: Go to **Settings > Privacy > Location Services** to see which apps have access to your location. You can choose to allow location access only while using an app, or disable it entirely for specific apps. Location Services is helpful for apps like maps and weather but can be turned off for apps that don't need it.
- **App Permissions**: In **Settings > Privacy**, you'll see options to manage permissions for photos, contacts, microphone, camera, and more. You can control which apps have access to these features, ensuring that only trusted apps can use them.
- **Tracking**: iOS 18 includes an **App Tracking Transparency** feature, which prompts apps to ask for your permission before tracking your activity across other apps and websites. This setting protects your privacy by limiting data sharing.

Apple has designed its devices to be accessible to everyone, regardless of physical abilities. iOS offers a range of accessibility options that can make the iPhone easier to use for individuals with vision, hearing, or mobility challenges.

- **VoiceOver**: VoiceOver is a screen reader that describes aloud what's happening on your screen. To enable VoiceOver, go to **Settings > Accessibility > VoiceOver**. This feature can be particularly helpful for users with low vision, as it provides spoken feedback for navigation and actions.
- **Magnifier**: Your iPhone can function as a digital magnifying glass with the **Magnifier** tool, found in **Settings > Accessibility > Magnifier**. This tool uses the camera to zoom in on objects or text, making it easier to see small details.
- **Hearing Aids and Sound Accessibility**: In **Settings > Accessibility > Hearing**, you'll find options for pairing compatible hearing aids and enabling audio enhancements for clearer sound during calls or while using media. You can also enable **Live Listen**, which uses your iPhone's microphone to amplify surrounding sounds directly to your AirPods or hearing aids.

To make sure your iPhone's battery lasts as long as possible, iOS 18 includes settings to manage power consumption.

- **Battery Health**: In **Settings > Battery > Battery Health**, you can view information about your battery's maximum capacity and check if it's in peak condition. You can also enable **Optimized Battery Charging**, which reduces battery aging by learning your charging habits and waiting to finish charging until you need it.
- **Low Power Mode**: If your battery is running low, you can activate **Low Power Mode** in **Settings > Battery**. This mode

reduces background activity and decreases performance slightly to extend battery life. It's useful if you're away from a charger and want to make sure your phone stays powered up as long as possible.

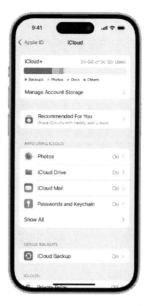

Your Apple ID and iCloud settings are central to managing your account, storage, and data sync across devices.

- **iCloud Storage**: In **Settings > [Your Name] > iCloud**, you can manage what data is stored in iCloud, including photos, contacts, and app data. iCloud syncs this data across all your Apple devices, so you always have access to your files.
- **Find My iPhone**: In **Settings > [Your Name] > Find My**, you can enable **Find My iPhone**. This feature lets you locate your device if it's lost and can even lock it remotely for security.

With these essential settings adjusted to fit your preferences, your iPhone is now optimized to provide a comfortable, secure, and enjoyable user experience. Taking a few moments to set up these options will save you time and ensure that your iPhone is tailored to suit your lifestyle and needs. Now, you're ready to start exploring more features and apps with confidence!

CHAPTER 2
BASIC NAVIGATION

Welcome to Basic Navigation! Now that your iPhone is set up and customized to your preferences, it's time to dive into the essentials of navigating the device. This chapter will introduce you to the layout of the iPhone 16, covering everything from understanding the Home Screen and Lock Screen to mastering the gestures and commands that make everyday use smooth and enjoyable. Getting comfortable with these basics is a great way to build confidence and efficiency with your new device.

Your iPhone's **Home Screen and Lock Screen** serve as the foundation of your experience. The Lock Screen is what you'll see first when you pick up your device, providing quick access to information like the time, date, and notifications, even before you unlock your phone. From here, you can use Face ID or a passcode to unlock the iPhone and access your Home Screen. The Home Screen is the main area where your apps are displayed, organized across several pages if you have many apps installed. We'll go over how to personalize the Home Screen layout and make it easier to find the apps you use most frequently.

In this chapter, we'll also explore **touch gestures**—swipes, taps, and pinches—that help you navigate the iPhone without needing physical buttons. Apple's gesture-based navigation might be new to you, especially if you're used to devices with more buttons, but it's designed to be intuitive and can quickly feel like second nature. For example, swiping up from the bottom of the screen takes you to the Home Screen, while swiping down from the top-right corner opens the Control Center, giving you easy access to settings like brightness and volume. We'll break down these gestures and explain how they simplify tasks on the iPhone.

One of the unique features of the iPhone 16 is the **Action Button**, which is a customizable button on the side of the device. This button allows you to quickly perform actions like muting your device, opening the camera, or enabling Do Not Disturb mode, depending on how you set it up. The Action Button can be adjusted to suit your needs, making it a powerful shortcut for the tasks you use most frequently.

We'll also introduce **Voice Commands** through Siri, Apple's voice assistant. Siri can be activated by pressing and holding the side button or simply saying "Hey Siri." With Siri, you can make calls, send messages, set reminders, and more without touching the screen. Voice commands are especially helpful if you need a hands-free way to perform tasks on your iPhone, and Siri is designed to understand a wide variety of requests.

Finally, we'll cover the **basics of calling, voicemail, and managing contacts**. Making and receiving calls is one of the primary functions of any phone, and we'll ensure you feel comfortable with the process on your iPhone. You'll learn how to access and organize your contacts, check voicemail, and set up favorites for easy access to the people you call most often.

By the end of this chapter, you'll be familiar with the main navigation tools on your iPhone, making it easier to use your device efficiently and confidently every day. Let's get started with these foundational navigation skills that will set you up for success with your new iPhone!

Home Screen and Lock Screen Overview

The **Home Screen** and **Lock Screen** are central to your iPhone 16 experience, acting as your gateway to all the apps, settings, and features on the device. Understanding how to navigate and customize these screens is key to using your iPhone efficiently and enjoying a smooth experience. This section will provide a detailed overview of the Home Screen and Lock Screen, covering how they work, how to personalize them, and some tips for making them more functional.

The Lock Screen is the first thing you see when you pick up your iPhone, and it gives you quick access to essential information and functions without needing to unlock the device. Here are some key elements and features of the Lock Screen:

- **Date, Time, and Notifications**: At the top of the Lock Screen, you'll see the current date and time. Any notifications, like text messages, missed calls, or app alerts, will appear below the time. You can tap on a notification to view more details or swipe to dismiss it if you don't need to interact with it.
- **Face ID and Unlocking**: The iPhone 16 uses Face ID for secure and convenient unlocking. Simply lift your iPhone and look at the screen; Face ID will recognize you and unlock the phone automatically. You'll see a small lock icon at the top, which will animate to an open position when Face ID successfully recognizes you. If Face ID isn't available or if you prefer, you can also unlock the iPhone by entering your passcode.
- **Quick Access Tools**: The Lock Screen provides shortcuts for quick access to essential tools:
  - » **Camera**: In the bottom-right corner, you'll see a camera icon. Press and hold this icon to instantly open the camera, allowing you to capture photos or videos quickly, even when your phone is locked.
  - » **Flashlight**: In the bottom-left corner, there's a flashlight icon. Press and hold this icon to turn on the flashlight, which is helpful for illuminating dark areas without needing to unlock your device or open the Control Center.
- **Notification Interactions**: Notifications on the Lock Screen are interactive. You can tap on a notification to open the corresponding app or swipe left to reveal additional options like "View" and "Clear." By swiping down on a notification and selecting "Clear All," you can remove all notifications at once, keeping your Lock Screen uncluttered.

The Lock Screen is designed to be functional and secure, providing you with quick access to essential features while protecting your information with Face ID or a passcode.

Tap to add widgets or change the clock's font.

The Lock Screen is customizable, allowing you to personalize the look and functionality according to your preferences. Here's how to customize some key elements:

- **Changing the Wallpaper**: To set a new wallpaper for your Lock Screen, go to **Settings > Wallpaper**. You'll have the option to choose from Apple's dynamic and still images or select a photo from your library. Choose an image that's easy on the eyes and aligns with your personal style. For a unique effect, you can enable **Perspective Zoom**, which creates a slight 3D effect as you tilt the phone.
- **Lock Screen Widgets**: With iOS 18, you can add widgets to your Lock Screen to display quick information, such as weather updates, calendar events, or reminders. To customize widgets, press and hold the Lock Screen until it enters edit mode, then tap on the widget area to add or remove widgets. These widgets are great for keeping important information visible without unlocking your iPhone.
- **Focus Modes**: Apple's Focus feature allows you to set specific Lock Screen configurations based on the time of day or your activity. For example, you can create a **Sleep Focus** that only shows essential notifications, or a **Work Focus** that highlights work-related apps. Go to **Settings > Focus** to set up different Focus modes that help you stay organized and minimize distractions.

By customizing the Lock Screen, you can create a personalized experience that offers quick access to the information and tools you need most often.

Once your iPhone is unlocked, you'll be greeted by the Home Screen, which is the primary interface where all your apps are displayed. The Home Screen layout is intuitive, and you can organize it to suit your needs. Here's an overview of the main features:

- **App Icons and Folders**: The Home Screen displays rows of app icons, arranged in a grid format. You can move app icons around by pressing and holding them until they start to jiggle, then dragging them to your preferred location. You can also create folders to organize apps by dragging one app icon over another, which automatically creates a new folder. Folders can be renamed to reflect the type of apps they contain, such as "Social" or "Productivity."
- **Dock**: At the bottom of the Home Screen, you'll see the Dock, a special area where you can place your most-used apps for quick access. The Dock remains the same across all Home Screen pages, making it easy to open frequently used apps from any screen. By default, the Dock includes apps like Phone, Messages, Safari, and Music, but you can customize it to include any apps you prefer.
- **Additional Home Screen Pages**: If you have many apps, they may span multiple Home Screen pages. You can swipe left and right to navigate between these pages. To add, remove, or rearrange Home Screen pages, press and hold an empty space on the Home Screen until the pages enter "jiggle" mode, then swipe through and make any desired adjustments.

Customizing the Home Screen allows you to create a layout that works for you. Here are some ways to personalize your Home Screen for a more user-friendly experience:

- **Widgets**: iOS 18 supports widgets on the Home Screen, which provide information at a glance without needing to open an app. For example, you can add a weather widget, a calendar widget, or a photos widget that displays recent pictures. To add widgets, press and hold an empty area on the Home Screen, tap the "+" icon in the top-left corner, and choose a widget from the list. You can resize and move widgets to any spot on the screen.

- **App Library**: If you prefer a minimalist look on your Home Screen, you can use the **App Library**, which organizes all your apps into categories. Swipe all the way to the right to access the App Library, where you'll find apps grouped by category, like Social, Entertainment, and Productivity. From here, you can remove apps from the Home Screen without deleting them entirely, keeping only the apps you use most visible.

- **Removing and Reinstalling Apps**: To remove an app from the Home Screen, press and hold its icon until a menu appears, then select "Remove App." You'll have the option to either delete the app entirely or remove it from the Home Screen while keeping it in the App Library. You can reinstall any app you've deleted by visiting the App Store and downloading it again.

Tap to add widgets or change the clock's font.

Here are some tips for making the most of your Home Screen and Lock Screen:

- **Quick Access with Spotlight Search**: Swipe down on the Home Screen to reveal **Spotlight Search**, which allows you to search for apps, contacts, emails, and more. This is especially helpful if you have many apps installed and want to find something quickly.

- **Control Center Access**: Swipe down from the top-right corner of the Home Screen or Lock Screen to open the **Control Center**, where you can adjust settings like brightness, volume, Wi-Fi, and Bluetooth. You can customize Control Center options in **Settings > Control Center** to add shortcuts for features like flashlight, calculator, and screen recording.
- **Dynamic Wallpapers**: For a more interactive experience, consider using a dynamic wallpaper on your Home Screen. Dynamic wallpapers are animated backgrounds that respond to the motion of your iPhone. You can choose one in **Settings > Wallpaper** for a touch of personalization and movement.

The Home Screen and Lock Screen are designed to make your iPhone easy to navigate and efficient to use. By understanding how to interact with these screens and customizing them to your preferences, you'll be able to access the features you need quickly and enjoy a more seamless experience with your iPhone. Now that you're familiar with the Home Screen and Lock Screen, you're ready to explore other ways to navigate and interact with your device!

Using Touch Gestures, Action Button, and Voice Commands

The iPhone 16 offers an intuitive way to interact with your device using a combination of touch gestures, the customizable Action Button, and Siri voice commands. These features are designed to make navigation fast, efficient, and accessible, eliminating the need for extensive physical buttons. In this section, we'll explore each of these input methods in detail, covering how they work and tips on using them effectively.

Touch gestures are the primary way to interact with your iPhone. By swiping, tapping, and pinching the screen, you can navigate through apps, access important settings, and manage tasks without physical buttons. Here are the most common gestures to know:

- **Swipe Up (Home Screen)**: Swiping up from the bottom of the screen is one of the most essential gestures on the iPhone 16. This action brings you back to the Home Screen from any app, allowing you to quickly access other apps or features. It replaces the need for a physical home button, and once you're accustomed to it, it becomes second nature.
- **Swipe Up and Hold (App Switcher)**: To switch between open apps, swipe up from the bottom of the screen and hold for a moment until you see the App Switcher, a carousel of recently used apps. From here, you can swipe left or right to browse apps, then tap an app to open it. If you want to close an app, simply swipe it up and off the screen in the App Switcher view.
- **Swipe Down from the Top Right (Control Center)**: The Control Center provides quick access to frequently used settings like Wi-Fi, Bluetooth, brightness, and volume controls. To open the Control Center, swipe down from the top-right corner of the screen. Here, you'll also find shortcuts for features like flashlight, calculator, and screen recording. You can customize Control Center shortcuts in **Settings > Control Center** to add or remove options based on your needs.

- **Swipe Down from the Middle (Spotlight Search)**: Spotlight Search is a powerful tool for finding apps, contacts, emails, and web results quickly. Swipe down from the middle of the Home Screen, and a search bar will appear at the top of the screen. Type in what you're looking for, and Spotlight will display relevant results instantly.
- **Swipe Left and Right (Home Screen Pages)**: If you have multiple Home Screen pages, swiping left and right will allow you to move between them. This gesture lets you easily navigate your apps and access additional pages with folders or widgets.
- **Pinch to Zoom**: In apps like Photos, Safari, and Maps, you can zoom in or out by placing two fingers on the screen and pinching them together (zoom out) or spreading them apart (zoom in). This gesture makes it easy to get a closer look at photos or read smaller text in web pages.
- **Double Tap**: A quick double-tap can be used in certain apps to zoom in, like in Photos or Safari. In other contexts, such as music or videos, a double-tap may also perform actions like pausing or playing content.
- **Haptic Touch**: By pressing and holding on certain items (like app icons or notifications), you'll trigger Haptic Touch, which provides additional options. For example, pressing an app icon can bring up quick actions related to the app, like creating a new message in the Messages app or setting an alarm in the Clock app.

These touch gestures make navigation on the iPhone smooth and efficient. They may take a bit of practice, especially if you're new to gesture-based controls, but once you're familiar with them, they make interacting with the device incredibly easy and fast.

The iPhone 16 introduces the **Action Button**, a new feature that provides quick access to your most-used actions. Located on the side of the iPhone where the mute switch used to be, the Action Button can be customized to trigger a variety of functions. This customizable button is designed to suit individual needs, making it an incredibly helpful shortcut. Here's how to make the most of it:

- **Customizing the Action Button**: To set up the Action Button, go to **Settings > Action Button**. Here, you'll find a list of functions that can be assigned to the button, including:
  - » **Mute/Unmute**: The default function, which mutes or unmutes your device.
  - » **Camera**: Launches the camera app, allowing you to capture photos and videos quickly.
  - » **Flashlight**: Turns on the flashlight, which is useful for illuminating dark spaces.
  - » **Do Not Disturb**: Activates Do Not Disturb mode, silencing calls and notifications.
  - » **Voice Memo**: Opens the Voice Memos app, allowing you to record audio notes instantly.
  - » **Shortcuts**: Assigning a shortcut lets you perform a wide range of tasks, such as sending a prewritten message or opening a specific app.
- **Using the Action Button**: Once you've customized the Action Button, simply press and hold it to activate the assigned function. This action is incredibly convenient for accessing commonly used tools without navigating through menus. For example, if you often take photos, setting the Action Button to open the camera app can save you time.

The Action Button adapts to your personal habits, allowing you to make the iPhone more tailored to your lifestyle. Whether you need a quick shortcut for tasks or simply want a dedicated mute button, the Action Button offers flexible options for enhanced usability.

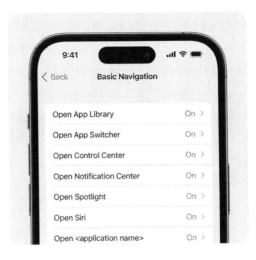

Siri, Apple's voice assistant, allows you to control many aspects of your iPhone using only your voice. This hands-free feature is perfect for situations where you may not be able to touch your phone, or if you simply prefer to give commands verbally. Siri can help with a wide variety of tasks, from setting reminders and making phone calls to searching the web and sending texts.

- **Activating Siri**: There are two ways to activate Siri on the iPhone 16:
  - » **Hey Siri**: If you've enabled "Hey Siri" during setup, you can simply say "Hey Siri" followed by your command. This option is useful for hands-free use and works even if your iPhone is locked.
  - » **Side Button**: Press and hold the side button to activate Siri. This is an alternative to "Hey Siri" and works well if you're in a noisy environment or prefer a button-activated option.
- **Common Siri Commands**:
  - » **Phone and Messaging**: You can say "Hey Siri, call [contact's name]" or "Hey Siri, send a text to [contact's name]" followed by your message. Siri will handle the rest, allowing you to make calls and send messages without touching the screen.
  - » **Reminders and Calendar**: Ask Siri to create reminders and calendar events, such as "Hey Siri, remind me to take my medication at 8 PM" or "Hey Siri, schedule an appointment with Dr. Smith for Monday at 10 AM." Siri will save the reminders and add calendar events automatically.
  - » **Weather and Directions**: Siri can provide quick answers to questions like "What's the weather like today?" or "How's the traffic to work?" It can also give directions, such as "Hey Siri, give me directions to the nearest coffee shop."
  - » **Information and Calculations**: Siri can answer general questions and perform calculations. Try asking, "Hey Siri, what's the capital of France?" or "Hey Siri, what's 25% of 200?"
  - » **Open Apps and Settings**: You can open apps and adjust settings with Siri by saying commands like "Hey Siri, open Notes" or "Hey Siri, turn on Bluetooth."
- **Customizing Siri's Responses**: You can adjust Siri's voice and response settings in **Settings > Siri & Search**. Here, you can choose Siri's voice, language, and decide when Siri responds out loud. You can also enable **Type to Siri**, allowing you to type commands instead of speaking, which is useful if you're in a quiet environment.

The iPhone 16's touch gestures, Action Button, and voice commands work together to offer a highly versatile experience. You can use these input methods independently or combine them for a smoother, faster way to navigate your device.

For instance, you might use touch gestures to browse your Home Screen and switch between apps, while setting the Action Button to activate the flashlight or camera for quick access. At the same time, you can rely on Siri to handle tasks like sending texts or setting reminders, allowing you to multitask and stay organized with minimal effort.

The combination of touch gestures, the Action Button, and Siri provides multiple options for interacting with your iPhone, allowing you to find the approach that feels most comfortable and efficient. By mastering these tools, you'll be able to make the most of your iPhone 16, whether you're new to smartphones or a seasoned user.

Basics of Calling, Voicemail, and Contacts

Your iPhone 16 makes it easy to stay connected with family, friends, and colleagues, whether by calling, leaving voicemails, or managing contact information. In this section, we'll cover the basics of making and receiving calls, setting up and using voicemail, and organizing contacts. By the end, you'll have a solid understanding of how to communicate effortlessly with your iPhone.

One of the main purposes of any phone, including the iPhone 16, is to make and receive calls. Apple has made this process user-friendly, and with a few taps, you'll be talking to your contacts in no time. Here's how to handle the basics of calling:

- **Making a Call**:
  - » Open the **Phone** app (the green icon with a white phone receiver) on your Home Screen or Dock.
  - » Tap on **Keypad** if you'd like to dial a number manually. Use the numbered keypad to enter the phone number, and then tap the green **Call** button to place the call.
  - » Alternatively, you can use the **Contacts** or **Recents** tabs within the Phone app. In **Contacts**, find the person you want to call and tap their name, then tap the phone icon next to their number to initiate the call. In **Recents**, you'll see a list of recent calls, and you can tap on any entry to call back.

- **Receiving a Call**: When someone calls you, your screen will display the caller's name or number if they're saved in your contacts. You'll have two main options:
  - » **Accept the Call**: Tap the green **Accept** button to answer the call. If your phone is locked when receiving the call, swipe up on the green button to answer.
  - » **Decline the Call**: Tap the red **Decline** button to send the call to voicemail. You can also press the side button on your iPhone to silence an incoming call without declining it.

- **Using Speakerphone and Mute**: During a call, you'll see several options on the screen, including **Speaker** and **Mute**:
  - » **Speaker**: Tap this to route the call's audio through the iPhone's external speaker, which is helpful if you need to be hands-free or if someone else wants to listen in on the conversation.
  - » **Mute**: Tapping Mute silences your microphone, so the other person won't hear any sound from your end. Tap again to unmute when you're ready to speak.

These basic functions ensure that you can start, receive, and manage calls easily, giving you control over your communications at every step.

Voicemail is a helpful feature that allows people to leave messages for you when you're unable to answer a call. Setting up voicemail on your iPhone is straightforward, and you can customize it with a personalized greeting. Here's how to set up and access your voicemail:

- **Setting Up Voicemail**:
  - » Open the **Phone** app and tap on the **Voicemail** tab at the bottom right of the screen. If this is your first time setting up voicemail, you'll see an option to **Set Up Now**.
  - » Tap **Set Up Now** and follow the prompts to create a voicemail password. You'll need this password to access your voicemail from other phones or for added security.
  - » After setting your password, you'll be prompted to record a greeting. You can choose **Default** (which plays a standard

greeting) or tap **Custom** to record a personalized message. If you choose Custom, follow the instructions to record your greeting and tap **Save** when done.

- **Listening to Voicemail Messages**:
  - » Go to the **Voicemail** tab in the Phone app to view a list of voicemail messages. Tap on any message to listen to it. You'll see the caller's name or number, the date and time of the message, and playback controls.
  - » Use the **Play** button to listen to the message, and tap **Speaker** if you'd like to hear it through the speaker rather than the earpiece.
  - » You can delete messages by swiping left on the message and tapping **Delete**, or you can tap the **Delete All** button to remove all voicemails at once. Deleted messages are moved to a Deleted Messages folder temporarily, so you can recover them if needed.
- **Visual Voicemail**: The iPhone's Visual Voicemail feature allows you to see a list of your voicemail messages, making it easy to pick and choose which messages to listen to without having to go through them in order. Some carriers even support voicemail transcription, so you can read a text version of the message if available. Check with your carrier to see if this feature is supported, as it can vary by provider.

Voicemail setup and management are designed to be easy on the iPhone, ensuring that you never miss important messages and can stay organized with your calls.

Your Contacts list is central to communicating efficiently on your iPhone. By organizing and maintaining a contacts list, you'll be able to call, message, and email people quickly and easily. Here's how to add, edit, and organize contacts on your iPhone:

- **Adding a New Contact**:
  - » Open the **Phone** app and go to the **Contacts** tab, then tap **+** in the top-right corner of the screen to add a new contact.
  - » Enter the person's information, such as their first and last name, phone number, and email address. You can also add additional details, like their address or birthday, by tapping **Add Field**.
  - » Tap **Done** to save the contact. The new contact will now appear in your Contacts list and can be accessed from the Phone app, Messages, or Mail.
- **Editing Contacts**:
  - » To update or edit a contact's information, go to **Contacts** in the Phone app and select the contact you want to edit. Tap **Edit** in the top-right corner to make changes.
  - » You can add new phone numbers, change email addresses, or update any other fields as needed. Tap **Done** when you're finished to save the changes.
- **Organizing Contacts with Favorites and Groups**:
  - » **Favorites**: Adding people to your Favorites list makes it easier to access them quickly. To add a contact to Favorites,

open their contact card, scroll down, and tap **Add to Favorites**. You can then choose whether you want to add them as a Favorite for calls, messages, or FaceTime. Favorites appear in the **Favorites** tab in the Phone app, allowing you to call or message frequently contacted people with a single tap.

» **Groups**: If you have a long list of contacts, organizing them into groups (such as "Family" or "Work") can make it easier to find specific people. While the iPhone's built-in Contacts app doesn't natively support creating groups, you can set up groups through iCloud on a computer, and they'll sync to your iPhone. To view a group, tap **Groups** in the Contacts tab of the Phone app and select the group you want to view.

- **Merging Duplicate Contacts**:

  » If you have multiple entries for the same person, you can merge these duplicates. In **Settings > Contacts**, enable **Contacts Found in Apps** to let iOS suggest duplicate contacts for merging. This feature will automatically prompt you to merge when it detects duplicate entries.

- **Using Siri with Contacts**:

  » Siri can also help you call or message contacts without manually opening the Contacts or Phone app. Say "Hey Siri, call [contact's name]" or "Hey Siri, send a message to [contact's name]," and Siri will handle the task for you. This is particularly useful if you're multitasking or need to be hands-free.

- **Blocking Unwanted Calls**: If you receive spam or unwanted calls, you can block these numbers. Go to the **Recents** tab in the Phone app, tap the information icon (an "i" in a circle) next to the unwanted number, and select **Block this Caller**.
- **Setting Up Emergency Contacts**: Adding emergency contacts to your iPhone can be helpful in critical situations. To set them up, open the **Health** app, tap your profile picture, then select **Medical ID**. You can add emergency contacts here, which first responders can access from your Lock Screen.
- **Personalized Ringtones for Contacts**: To make certain contacts stand out, you can assign custom ringtones. Go to the contact card, tap **Edit**, and select **Ringtone**. Choose a unique ringtone so you can immediately recognize calls from specific people.

With these calling, voicemail, and contact management basics, you'll be able to handle communications smoothly and efficiently on your iPhone 16. Whether you're making calls, organizing contacts, or customizing settings to match your preferences, the iPhone's tools make it easy to stay connected in a way that's both convenient and enjoyable.

CHAPTER 3
CUSTOMIZATION

Welcome to Chapter 3: Customization! Now that you're familiar with navigating your iPhone 16, it's time to make it truly your own. Customization is all about adjusting your device to suit your preferences and lifestyle. This chapter will cover everything from adjusting the display brightness, text size, and sound settings to personalizing ringtones, wallpapers, and widgets, as well as exploring accessibility options that enhance comfort and ease of use. These settings allow you to tailor your iPhone experience, making it more enjoyable, user-friendly, and unique.

The **display** settings give you control over how things look and feel on your iPhone, allowing you to change the brightness level, text size, and overall display style. You can make text larger or bolder for easier reading, set up Dark Mode for a softer, darker screen, and even adjust the color balance to make the display more comfortable on your eyes. These options ensure that you can see everything clearly, even in different lighting conditions.

In addition to display settings, **sound customization** offers you the ability to adjust how your iPhone notifies you. You can personalize ringtones for specific contacts, set custom text tones, and even select distinct sounds for other alerts. These small touches make it easier to recognize important calls and messages right away. Customizing your sound settings is an easy way to add personality to your iPhone, allowing you to identify each notification with a unique tone.

One of the most exciting ways to customize your iPhone is through **wallpapers and widgets**. Wallpapers let you change the background image on both the Home and Lock screens, so you can see a favorite photo or design every time you unlock your phone. Widgets, on the other hand, provide quick access to essential information like weather, calendar events, or reminders right on your Home Screen. With iOS 18, you can even resize and rearrange widgets, making it easy to view what matters most at a glance.

For those who want an even more personalized experience, **accessibility settings** offer additional options that make the iPhone more comfortable and easier to use. Whether you have specific visual, hearing, or physical needs, Apple's accessibility features include options like VoiceOver, Magnifier, and hearing aid compatibility to ensure your iPhone works with you. These features are designed to improve comfort and usability, making the iPhone accessible to everyone.

This chapter will walk you through each of these customization options, helping you set up your iPhone so that it reflects your style, meets your needs, and feels uniquely yours. By the end of this chapter, you'll know how to make your iPhone an extension of yourself, with personalized settings that make it easier and more enjoyable to use every day. Let's dive in and start customizing!

Adjusting Display Brightness, Text Size, and Sound

Customizing the display brightness, text size, and sound on your iPhone 16 is a simple yet impactful way to make your device feel more personal and comfortable. These settings allow you to tailor the screen visibility and sound to fit different environments, from low-light spaces to outdoor settings, and to make text easier to read. Here, we'll walk through how to adjust each of these settings and provide some helpful tips to enhance your viewing and listening experience.

The brightness level on your iPhone's screen determines how easy it is to see and read content, and adjusting it properly can also help preserve battery life. Here's how to customize brightness settings:

- **Manual Brightness Adjustment**:
  - » Open **Settings** and go to **Display & Brightness**.
  - » You'll see a slider under **Brightness**—move it to the right to increase brightness or to the left to reduce it. For daytime outdoor use, higher brightness will make the screen easier to see in sunlight, while lower brightness can be more comfortable indoors or in dark environments.

- **Auto-Brightness**:
  - » Auto-Brightness adjusts the brightness level automatically based on your surrounding light conditions, reducing strain on your eyes and helping to save battery life. To enable or disable Auto-Brightness, go to **Settings > Accessibility > Display & Text Size**, then toggle **Auto-Brightness** on or off.
  - » When Auto-Brightness is turned on, your iPhone will automatically adjust the screen brightness depending on whether you're in a bright or dim environment. This feature can be particularly useful if you frequently switch between indoor and outdoor use.

- **Night Shift and True Tone**:
  - » **Night Shift** is a feature that changes the screen color to a warmer tone in the evening, reducing blue light that can interfere with sleep. To enable Night Shift, go to **Settings > Display & Brightness > Night Shift**. You can set it to turn on automatically from sunset to sunrise or schedule specific hours.
  - » **True Tone** adjusts the color temperature based on ambient lighting, making the display appear more natural. For example, in warm light, the screen will have a slightly warmer color, while in cooler light, it will appear cooler. Enable True Tone in **Settings > Display & Brightness** for a display that adapts to your surroundings for comfortable viewing.

By adjusting brightness, Night Shift, and True Tone settings, you can make your iPhone's display more comfortable to view across various lighting conditions.

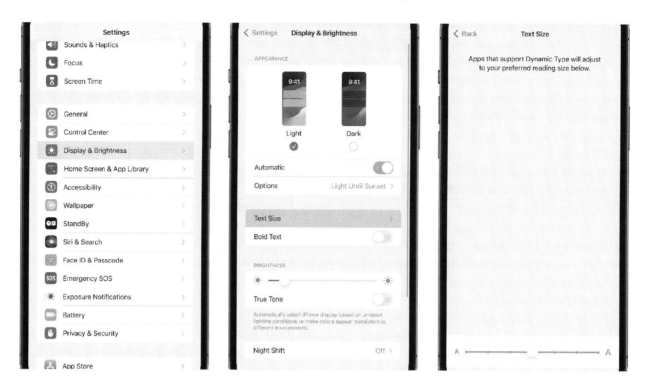

If you prefer larger or bolder text for easier reading, your iPhone provides flexible options to adjust the display text size and appearance. Here's how to customize text settings to make reading more comfortable:

- **Adjusting Text Size**:
  - » Go to **Settings > Display & Brightness > Text Size**. Here, you'll find a slider that lets you increase or decrease the text size.
  - » Moving the slider to the right will enlarge the text, which can be helpful for anyone with vision difficulties or for reading small text in emails, messages, and web pages.
- **Bold Text**:
  - » To make text appear bolder across all apps and settings, go to **Settings > Display & Brightness** and toggle on **Bold Text**. This option increases text thickness, making it stand out more prominently, which can enhance readability.
- **Zoom Display**:
  - » The iPhone offers a **Display Zoom** feature that makes icons and text appear larger. This is particularly helpful if you find the default interface size a bit small. Go to **Settings > Display & Brightness** and select **View (Display Zoom)**.
  - » Choose **Standard** for the normal display view or **Zoomed** for a larger view of icons and text, then tap **Set** to apply your preference.
- **Reduce Motion and Increase Contrast**:
  - » Reducing motion effects, like screen transitions and animations, can make your display feel more stable and may help with visual comfort. To reduce motion, go to **Settings > Accessibility > Motion** and toggle on **Reduce Motion**.
  - » You can also increase contrast to make text and buttons more defined. In **Settings > Accessibility > Display & Text Size**, enable **Increase Contrast** for a higher contrast between background and text.

Adjusting text size and display settings allows you to create a more personalized and readable experience on your iPhone, ensuring that reading and navigating are comfortable.

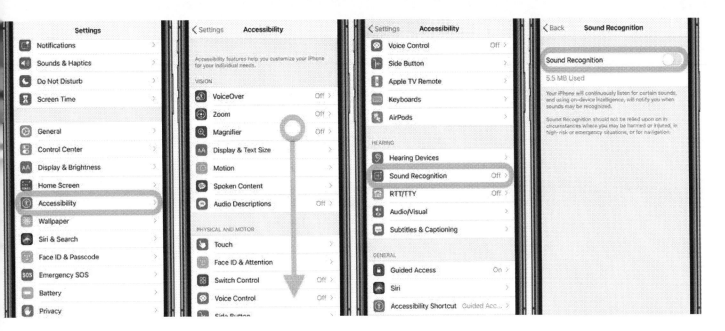

The sound settings on your iPhone allow you to adjust volume levels, choose ringtones, and customize alerts to fit your preferences. Here's how to manage sound settings effectively:

- **Volume Control**:

  » Your iPhone has separate volume settings for **Ringer and Alerts** and for **Media** (like music and videos).

  » To adjust the **Ringer and Alerts** volume, go to **Settings > Sounds & Haptics** and use the slider under **Ringer and Alerts**. You can also enable **Change with Buttons** to adjust the ringer volume using the physical volume buttons on the side of your iPhone.

  » **Media Volume** can be adjusted when playing music, videos, or other media by using the volume buttons on the side of the device. The on-screen volume indicator will show whether you're adjusting the ringer or media volume based on the context.

- **Ringtones and Alert Sounds**:

  » To customize your ringtone, go to **Settings > Sounds & Haptics** and tap **Ringtone**. You'll see a list of default ringtones as well as any ringtones you've purchased or downloaded.

  » For text messages, emails, and other notifications, you can customize alert sounds under **Settings > Sounds & Haptics**. Tap on the specific alert type (like **Text Tone** or **New Mail**) to choose a unique sound for each. Custom alert sounds help you identify different notifications instantly.

- **Vibration Patterns**:

  » If you'd like additional customization, your iPhone allows you to create custom vibration patterns. Go to **Settings > Sounds & Haptics**, select **Ringtone** or any other alert type, then tap **Vibration**. Choose **Create New Vibration** to tap out a custom vibration pattern, which will be saved and applied to that specific alert.

  » Custom vibrations can be particularly helpful if you often keep your phone on silent mode but still want to distinguish between different types of alerts.

- **Haptics (Vibration Feedback)**:

  » Haptic feedback refers to subtle vibrations that accompany certain actions, like typing on the keyboard or interacting with apps. You can manage haptic feedback settings in **Settings > Sounds & Haptics** by toggling **System Haptics** on or off.

  » Enabling haptics can make your iPhone feel more interactive, as you'll get small, satisfying vibrations with each tap or action. However, if you prefer a quieter experience or want to conserve battery life, you may choose to disable this feature.

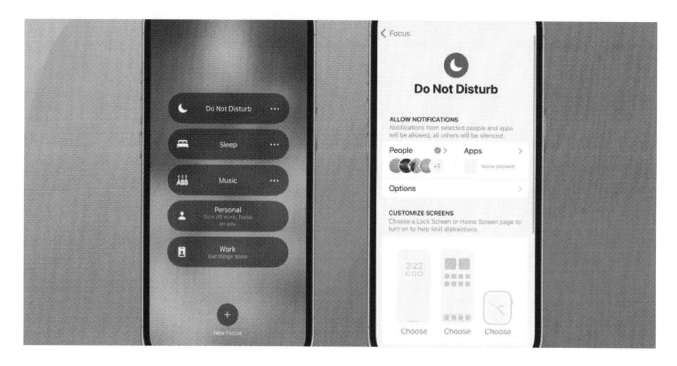

Your iPhone has options to control sound and notification interruptions, especially helpful for situations when you need peace and quiet, like meetings or bedtime:

- **Silent Mode**:
    - » To quickly silence your iPhone, flip the **Ring/Silent switch** on the side of the device. When Silent Mode is enabled, your iPhone won't make any sound for incoming calls or notifications, though it will still vibrate if vibration is on.
    - » You'll see an orange indicator on the switch when Silent Mode is active. Flip the switch back to return to normal sound mode.

- **Do Not Disturb and Focus Modes**:
    - » **Do Not Disturb** is part of the Focus modes in iOS, which allow you to control when and which notifications come through. Go to **Settings > Focus > Do Not Disturb** to set up Do Not Disturb mode.
    - » You can customize it to allow calls from specific contacts, repeat calls, or enable notifications from certain apps. This feature is useful if you want to limit distractions without silencing important notifications entirely.
    - » For even more control, explore other Focus modes like **Work** or **Sleep** in **Settings > Focus**. Each mode can have unique settings, so you can adjust notifications depending on your activities.

Your iPhone 16 supports a range of headphones and audio accessories, including Bluetooth headphones, like Apple's AirPods, and traditional wired headphones using an adapter. Here's how to manage sound with these accessories:

- **Connecting Bluetooth Headphones**:
  - » Go to **Settings > Bluetooth** and make sure Bluetooth is turned on. Put your headphones in pairing mode (consult your headphone's manual if you're unsure how), and they should appear in the list of available devices. Tap on them to connect.
  - » Once connected, your iPhone will automatically route all audio, like calls and media, through the headphones. You can manage the audio volume using the iPhone's volume buttons or the controls on the headphones if they have them.
- **Customizing Headphone Audio**:
  - » For compatible headphones, you can adjust audio settings under **Settings > Accessibility > Audio/Visual**. Enable **Headphone Accommodations** to customize sound levels and frequencies to suit your hearing preferences. This is particularly helpful if you need enhanced audio clarity for speech or music.

By adjusting display brightness, text size, and sound settings, you'll make your iPhone easier and more comfortable to use in any environment. These settings are the foundation of a customized iPhone experience, allowing you to see, hear, and interact with your device exactly how you like it. With these basics in place, your iPhone is ready to perform at its best, whether you're reading, listening, or simply enjoying your personalized device.

Personalizing Ringtones, Wallpapers, and Widgets

Customizing ringtones, wallpapers, and widgets on your iPhone 16 is a great way to make your device feel uniquely yours. These personalization options allow you to create a more enjoyable and functional experience, from setting custom tones for contacts to displaying useful information on your Home Screen. In this section, we'll walk through each aspect of personalization in detail, covering how to set up unique ringtones, choose and change wallpapers, and add widgets that make accessing important information quick and easy.

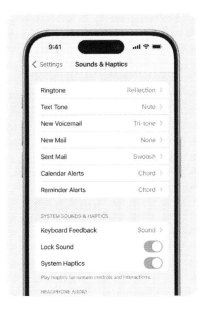

Your iPhone's ringtone is one of the most noticeable aspects of personalization. Setting a unique ringtone for calls, texts, and specific contacts helps you recognize who's calling or messaging without even looking at the screen. Here's how to customize these sounds:

- **Changing the Default Ringtone**:
  - » Go to **Settings > Sounds & Haptics**. Tap on **Ringtone** to see a list of available sounds. iPhone includes several default ringtones, from classic options like "Marimba" to newer tones. Simply tap on a ringtone to hear a preview and select it as your default tone.

» If you prefer something more unique, scroll down and tap **Tone Store** to browse the iTunes Store for additional ringtones. These can be purchased and downloaded directly to your iPhone for a wider selection.

- **Setting Custom Text Tones and Alert Sounds**:
    » In **Settings > Sounds & Haptics**, you can also customize the sound for **Text Tone**, **New Mail**, **Sent Mail**, and other alerts. This allows you to assign unique sounds for each type of notification, making it easier to differentiate them.
    » Just like with ringtones, you can purchase additional text tones from the Tone Store if you want more options.

- **Assigning Ringtones to Specific Contacts**:
    » To personalize ringtones for individual contacts, open the **Contacts** app and select the contact you'd like to customize. Tap **Edit** in the top right corner, then scroll down to **Ringtone**. Here, you can assign a unique ringtone for calls from this contact, which is especially helpful for family members or frequently contacted people.
    » You can also set a custom **Text Tone** for the contact in the same menu, allowing you to immediately recognize messages from important contacts.

- **Creating Custom Vibration Patterns**:
    » If you frequently keep your iPhone on silent or vibrate, creating custom vibration patterns can help you distinguish between different types of notifications. In **Settings > Sounds & Haptics**, tap **Ringtone** or **Text Tone**, then select **Vibration**. From here, choose **Create New Vibration** and tap out a pattern that will play each time you receive a call or text from a specific contact.
    » This feature is especially useful for those who rely on vibration feedback, as it provides another layer of customization without sound.

By personalizing your ringtones, text tones, and vibrations, you can create a more organized and recognizable sound experience that keeps you aware of who's contacting you and what type of notification you're receiving.

Wallpapers are a quick and easy way to give your iPhone a fresh look. You can set different wallpapers for the Home Screen and Lock Screen, allowing you to see a favorite photo, a design, or a calming image every time you unlock your phone. Here's how to choose and set your wallpapers:

- **Selecting a Wallpaper**:
    » Go to **Settings > Wallpaper**, then tap **Choose a New Wallpaper**. You'll see a selection of Apple's default wallpapers, including **Dynamic**, **Still**, and **Live** options:

    Dynamic wallpapers have gentle moving patterns.

    Still wallpapers are static images, and Apple offers a variety of themes, including landscapes and abstract designs.

    Live wallpapers animate briefly when you press and hold the screen (available on certain iPhone models).

»   You can also select a wallpaper from your **Photos** library. If you have a favorite photo of family, friends, or a beautiful scene, choosing it as your wallpaper brings a personal touch.

Setting Wallpapers for Home Screen and Lock Screen:

»   Once you choose a wallpaper, you'll see a preview screen. You can adjust the position and zoom level by pinching to zoom in or out. When you're satisfied, tap **Set** and choose whether you'd like the wallpaper to appear on the **Lock Screen**, **Home Screen**, or **Both**.

»   Setting different wallpapers for the Lock and Home Screens allows you to enjoy variety and creates a visually dynamic experience each time you unlock your phone.

Using Perspective Zoom and Depth Effects:

»   Some wallpapers support **Perspective Zoom**, a feature that creates a subtle 3D effect as you tilt your phone, adding a sense of depth to the background image. You can enable or disable Perspective Zoom on the preview screen by tapping the button at the bottom.

»   With iOS 18, **Depth Effects** use advanced processing to create layered images where icons or widgets appear as if they're above or behind the wallpaper. This feature is available on compatible images and adds an extra layer of visual appeal.

Wallpapers are one of the simplest ways to personalize your iPhone, giving it a look that reflects your style and interests. Changing your wallpaper periodically can keep your device feeling fresh and new.

Widgets are a practical way to access important information on your Home Screen without needing to open individual apps. With iOS 18, widgets are more customizable and interactive, letting you view information, track tasks, and even interact with some app functions. Here's how to add and customize widgets:

Adding a Widget to the Home Screen:

»   To add a widget, press and hold an empty area on the Home Screen until the apps begin to jiggle. Tap the **+** icon in the top-left corner of the screen to open the widget gallery.

»   Scroll through the available widgets, which are organized by app, and select one that interests you, such as **Weather**, **Calendar**, **Reminders**, or **Photos**. Tap on the widget to see available size options (small, medium, or large), then tap **Add Widget** to place it on the Home Screen.

Customizing Widget Placement and Size:

»   Once a widget is on the Home Screen, you can move it by pressing and holding until it jiggles, then dragging it to your preferred location. You can also change the size of some widgets in the widget gallery before adding them.

»   Larger widgets display more information but take up more space, while smaller widgets are compact and fit neatly among your app icons.

- **Widget Stacks and Smart Stacks**:
  - » **Widget Stacks** allow you to layer multiple widgets on top of each other, making it easy to scroll through different widgets in the same location. To create a stack, drag one widget on top of another of the same size, and they will combine into a stack that you can scroll through.
  - » **Smart Stack** is a pre-designed widget stack that uses Siri intelligence to show you relevant widgets based on your activity, location, and time of day. For example, it might show you Calendar events in the morning, News in the afternoon, and Fitness data in the evening. You can add a Smart Stack from the widget gallery and customize its settings to control which widgets appear.
- **Editing Widget Settings**:
  - » Many widgets offer customization options to display specific information. For example, you can set a weather widget to show your preferred location or a calendar widget to display only certain calendars. To edit a widget, press and hold it, then tap **Edit Widget**. Make any desired changes, then tap **Done**.

Widgets make the Home Screen more functional by providing glanceable information and interactive elements that keep you informed. By carefully choosing and arranging widgets, you can create a Home Screen layout that meets your needs and makes essential information easily accessible.

- **Balance Widgets and App Icons**: When adding widgets, consider the layout of your Home Screen. Balance widget sizes with app icons so that your screen remains organized and visually appealing.
- **Match Wallpaper and Widget Themes**: For a cohesive look, try selecting wallpapers and widget colors that complement each other. Some widgets, like the Clock or Weather, adapt their colors based on the wallpaper to maintain visual harmony.
- **Update Seasonally or by Mood**: Changing wallpapers and widgets seasonally or based on your mood is a fun way to keep your iPhone feeling fresh. Try a vibrant wallpaper in summer and a more subdued one in winter, or switch up widgets based on your current priorities.

Personalizing ringtones, wallpapers, and widgets is a quick yet effective way to make your iPhone truly yours. By following these steps, you'll create a device that's not only functional but also reflects your personality and style. With these customizations, each interaction with your iPhone becomes more enjoyable, from hearing a familiar tone to viewing useful widgets and a favorite wallpaper. Enjoy making your iPhone as unique as you are!

Accessibility Options for Comfort and Ease

Apple has designed the iPhone 16 with a range of accessibility features that make the device more comfortable and easy to use for everyone, especially those with specific needs related to vision, hearing, physical and motor skills, and cognitive support. These accessibility options provide customizable solutions, allowing you to adjust the iPhone interface and interac-

...tions to fit your comfort and preferences. In this section, we'll explore the accessibility features in detail, guiding you through setup and providing tips to help you make the most of each setting.

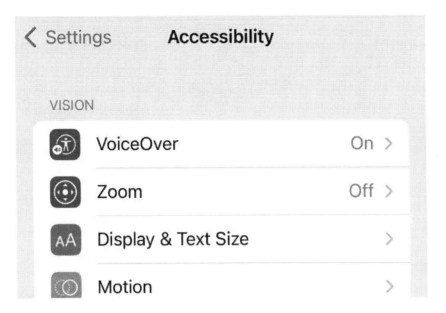

For those who have low vision or simply prefer larger and clearer text and visuals, the iPhone offers several options to enhance readability and interaction. Here's a look at the key vision-related features:

- **VoiceOver**:
  - » **VoiceOver** is a powerful screen reader that narrates what's happening on your iPhone screen, from reading out text to describing icons and apps. To enable VoiceOver, go to **Settings > Accessibility > VoiceOver** and toggle it on.
  - » VoiceOver is gesture-based, allowing you to tap and swipe to hear descriptions of items on the screen. Once enabled, double-tapping selects an item, while a single tap reads out its description. This feature is invaluable for users with visual impairments and can be customized with different voices, speaking rates, and verbosity levels.
- **Zoom**:
  - » The **Zoom** feature magnifies your iPhone's display, allowing you to enlarge sections of the screen for better readability. You can enable Zoom in **Settings > Accessibility > Zoom**. Once active, double-tapping with three fingers allows you to zoom in and out.
  - » You can adjust the zoom level, move around the screen using three fingers, and choose **Window Zoom** (which magnifies only part of the screen) or **Full-Screen Zoom**. Zoom provides an extra layer of flexibility, especially when reading small text or viewing detailed content.
- **Display and Text Size Options**:
  - » In **Settings > Accessibility > Display & Text Size**, you'll find options to make text larger, bolder, and even increase contrast for better visibility. Here are some helpful settings:

  Larger Text: Enables larger text sizes across apps, making it easier to read menus, messages, and content.

  Bold Text: Adds thickness to text for enhanced readability.

  Increase Contrast: Adds more contrast between text and backgrounds for improved clarity.

  Color Filters: For those with color blindness, Color Filters adjust colors to accommodate different visual needs.
- **Magnifier**:
  - » The **Magnifier** turns your iPhone into a digital magnifying glass, using the camera to zoom in on objects or text. Enable it in **Settings > Accessibility > Magnifier**, then triple-click the side button to activate. This feature is perfect for reading small print on documents, labels, or menus.
- **Speak Screen and Speak Selection**:
  - » These features read text aloud from documents, web pages, and apps. Go to **Settings > Accessibility > Spoken**

Content to enable **Speak Selection** (which reads selected text) and **Speak Screen** (which reads the entire screen). Swipe down with two fingers from the top of the screen to start Speak Screen.

These vision accessibility features make reading, navigating, and interacting with the iPhone easier and more enjoyable for users with low vision or reading challenges.

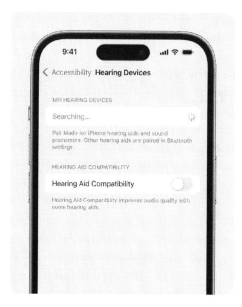

Apple has integrated several tools to support those with hearing impairments, including options for compatible hearing aids, sound customization, and visual alerts:

- **Hearing Aid Compatibility**:

  » The iPhone 16 is compatible with MFi (Made for iPhone) hearing aids, allowing direct audio streaming and sound adjustments for supported devices. Go to **Settings > Accessibility > Hearing Devices** to connect and customize settings for your hearing aids.

  » With connected hearing aids, you can control volume levels, choose specific audio programs, and monitor battery life directly from your iPhone.

- **Sound Recognition**:

  » **Sound Recognition** listens for specific sounds, like doorbells, smoke alarms, or crying babies, and sends you an alert if it detects them. This feature is especially useful for users with hearing impairments who might miss important sounds. To set up Sound Recognition, go to **Settings > Accessibility > Sound Recognition** and choose which sounds you'd like your iPhone to recognize.

- **Mono Audio and Balance Control**:

  » **Mono Audio** combines stereo sound channels into a single channel, ensuring that all audio can be heard through one ear. This feature is helpful for users who have better hearing in one ear. You can enable Mono Audio in **Settings > Accessibility > Audio/Visual**.

  » **Balance Control** allows you to adjust audio levels between the left and right speakers or headphones, helping to create a balanced audio experience based on your specific hearing needs.

- **Live Listen**:

  » With **Live Listen**, your iPhone acts as a remote microphone, sending amplified sound directly to your AirPods or hearing aids. This feature is helpful for improving clarity in conversations in noisy environments. Enable Live Listen in **Settings > Control Center** by adding the **Hearing** control, then turn on Live Listen when needed.

- **Subtitles and Closed Captions**:

  » In **Settings > Accessibility > Subtitles & Captioning**, you can enable closed captions or subtitles for supported media content. You can also customize the appearance of subtitles to make them easier to read by adjusting font size, color, and background opacity.

Hearing accessibility features ensure that iPhone users can fully enjoy audio and visual content, communicate clearly, and receive essential alerts, enhancing their overall experience.

For users with limited physical and motor skills, the iPhone includes options to make interaction more accessible. These features are customizable to suit individual mobility needs and preferences:

- **AssistiveTouch**:
  - » **AssistiveTouch** is a customizable on-screen menu that allows you to perform actions, such as tapping, swiping, or pressing buttons, without physically interacting with the device. To enable it, go to **Settings > Accessibility > Touch > AssistiveTouch**.
  - » Once enabled, a floating AssistiveTouch button appears on the screen. Tapping it opens a menu with shortcuts for Home, Siri, Volume Control, and more. You can customize these shortcuts to fit your needs, making it easier to access frequently used actions.

- **Back Tap**:
  - » **Back Tap** is a feature that lets you perform actions by double-tapping or triple-tapping the back of your iPhone. To set it up, go to **Settings > Accessibility > Touch > Back Tap** and choose actions for double or triple taps, such as opening the Control Center, taking a screenshot, or launching a specific app.
  - » This feature is convenient for performing quick tasks without needing to reach for on-screen controls.

- **Switch Control**:
  - » **Switch Control** allows you to use adaptive devices (such as switches or a joystick) to interact with the iPhone, providing an alternative to touch-based input. You can enable Switch Control in **Settings > Accessibility > Switch Control**.
  - » Once enabled, Switch Control lets you navigate through items on the screen with a switch or other adaptive device, highlighting each item in sequence. When the desired item is highlighted, pressing the switch selects it, providing hands-free access to iPhone features.

- **Touch Accommodations**:
  - » **Touch Accommodations** adjust how the screen responds to touches, helpful for users with limited dexterity or motor control. Go to **Settings > Accessibility > Touch > Touch Accommodations** to enable features like **Hold Duration** (which requires holding a touch for a specific time) or **Ignore Repeat** (which ignores multiple taps in quick succession).
  - » These settings can be customized to reduce accidental actions and provide more control over touch interactions.

Physical and motor accessibility features ensure that users with mobility challenges can navigate and interact with their iPhone with ease and independence.

For users with cognitive or learning disabilities, Apple offers settings that simplify the iPhone experience, providing clear layouts and minimizing distractions:

- **Guided Access**:
    - » **Guided Access** limits iPhone use to a single app and restricts certain areas of the screen, which is helpful for staying focused on a task. Enable it in **Settings > Accessibility > Guided Access**.
    - » Once enabled, triple-click the side button within any app to start Guided Access. You can disable areas of the screen that should not be touched, set a time limit, or require a passcode to exit the app, making it easier to concentrate on a single task.

- **Siri Suggestions and Focus**:
    - » Siri can suggest actions based on your habits, such as suggesting shortcuts for frequently used apps or routines. In **Settings > Siri & Search**, you can enable **Siri Suggestions** to help guide you through daily tasks. Siri can also provide reminders based on your location or time of day.
    - » **Focus** is another helpful tool that filters notifications based on specific activities, like work or relaxation. Set up Focus in **Settings > Focus** to create custom modes that prioritize the apps and people you want notifications from, reducing unnecessary distractions.

- **Reduce Motion and Visual Clarity**:
    - » For users who may experience discomfort with screen animations, **Reduce Motion** reduces visual effects on the iPhone, making navigation smoother. Go to **Settings > Accessibility > Motion** and enable **Reduce Motion**.
    - » **Reduce Transparency** in **Settings > Accessibility > Display & Text Size** adds clarity to screen backgrounds, making icons and text more prominent.

These features make it easier for individuals with cognitive or learning needs to use the iPhone by providing focused, simplified, and distraction-free interfaces.

Apple's accessibility options on the iPhone 16 ensure that the device is usable, comfortable, and empowering for everyone, regardless of their specific needs. By exploring these features, you can personalize your iPhone to create a more enjoyable and supportive experience, allowing you to communicate, navigate, and interact with ease and independence. Whether you use just one or many of these settings, accessibility options provide valuable tools that make your iPhone a device that works with you, on your terms.

CHAPTER 4
BUILT-IN APPS FOR DAILY LIFE

Welcome to Chapter 4: Built-In Apps for Daily Life! Your iPhone 16 comes pre-loaded with a suite of built-in apps designed to make everyday tasks more convenient and enjoyable. From capturing special moments with the camera to keeping track of appointments and reminders, these apps are powerful tools that help you organize, document, and manage your day-to-day activities. In this chapter, we'll explore the essentials of these apps, guiding you through their functions and how to make the most of them in your daily life.

One of the most popular features on the iPhone is the **Camera** app, which is both powerful and easy to use. Whether you're taking photos of family gatherings, snapping quick shots of your garden, or capturing scenic moments on vacation, the Camera app offers everything you need to get great pictures. In this section, we'll start with the basics of taking photos and videos, adjusting settings, and viewing your captured memories in the Photos app. You'll also learn a few helpful tips to make your photos look their best and discover ways to organize and share them with family and friends.

Next, we'll dive into three of the iPhone's most versatile and useful apps: **Notes, Calendar, and Clock**. The **Notes** app is perfect for jotting down quick ideas, shopping lists, or even saving important documents with its built-in scanning feature. The **Calendar** app helps you keep track of appointments, family events, and personal goals, making it easy to stay organized and never miss an important date. Meanwhile, the **Clock** app offers a variety of tools, from setting alarms and timers to tracking world time zones, so you can manage your time effectively. Each of these apps is straightforward to use, and in this chapter, we'll cover their essential features to help you incorporate them into your daily routines.

Finally, we'll explore how to set up **Reminders and Tasks** on your iPhone. The **Reminders** app is an excellent tool for managing to-do lists, setting reminders for tasks, and organizing errands. Whether you're planning to pick up groceries, schedule a doctor's appointment, or simply remember to call a friend, the Reminders app ensures that no task slips through the cracks. You can set up reminders with specific times, dates, or even locations, giving you control over how and when you're notified.

This chapter is all about helping you integrate these built-in apps into your daily life with ease. By the end of this chapter, you'll feel confident using the Camera app to capture and relive moments, organizing your schedule with Notes, Calendar, and Clock, and managing daily tasks with the Reminders app. These tools are designed to simplify everyday activities and keep you connected and organized. Let's dive in and discover how these built-in apps can make a difference in your daily life, adding convenience, fun, and structure to your routines!

Camera Basics: Taking and Viewing Photos

The iPhone 16's Camera app is one of its most impressive features, offering a powerful tool for capturing life's moments with ease. Whether you're documenting family gatherings, capturing stunning landscapes, or taking quick snapshots of daily life, the iPhone's Camera app provides excellent photo quality and a wide range of features to enhance your photography experience. This section will guide you through the basics of taking photos and videos, adjusting camera settings, and viewing and organizing your images in the Photos app.

The Camera app on the iPhone 16 is designed to be user-friendly, with intuitive controls that make taking photos simple, even for beginners. Here's how to get started:

- **Opening the Camera App**: You can access the Camera app directly from the Home Screen by tapping on the Camera icon, or from the Lock Screen by swiping left or pressing the camera icon in the bottom-right corner. These options ensure that you can quickly open the camera and capture a moment without delay.
- **Familiarizing Yourself with the Layout**: When you open the Camera app, you'll see several icons and controls on the screen. Along the bottom, you'll find mode options (Photo, Video, Portrait, etc.), and at the top, you'll see settings icons, including Flash, Live Photos, and HDR. Familiarizing yourself with this layout helps you quickly access the tools you need while taking photos.

The Camera app offers multiple modes, each designed for specific types of photography. Here's an overview of the main modes and how to use them:

- **Photo Mode**: This is the default mode for taking standard photos. Simply point your iPhone at your subject, adjust the focus and exposure by tapping on the screen where you want the focus, and press the shutter button (the large circle at the bottom center of the screen) to capture the image. Photo mode is perfect for everyday snapshots and general photography.
- **Portrait Mode**: Portrait mode is designed for taking photos with a professional-looking background blur (known as "bokeh"). It works best when photographing people or objects with a distinct subject that you want to stand out. To use

Portrait mode, swipe to the Portrait option in the Camera app, position your subject within the frame, and wait for the camera to apply the background blur effect before pressing the shutter.

- **Video Mode**: For recording videos, swipe to the Video mode in the Camera app. Press the red record button to start recording and tap it again to stop. Video mode allows you to capture high-quality video, perfect for documenting events, activities, and special moments. You can also adjust the resolution and frame rate in **Settings > Camera > Record Video** for more control over video quality.
- **Panorama Mode**: Panorama mode is ideal for capturing wide, scenic views, like landscapes or cityscapes. In this mode, you'll move your iPhone in a horizontal line across the scene you want to capture. The camera will stitch the images together into a single, wide photo. To use Panorama mode, select it from the mode options, press the shutter button, and follow the on-screen guidance to move your phone steadily across the scene.
- **Night Mode**: Night mode activates automatically in low-light settings, allowing you to take clear photos without flash. When Night mode is active, you'll see a moon icon on the screen, and the camera will suggest a recommended exposure time. Hold your phone steady or use a tripod, as Night mode may take a few seconds to capture the photo, improving image quality in dark environments.

Each mode offers unique advantages, and experimenting with them can help you capture different styles of photos, from portraits to landscapes and night scenes.

The Camera app includes several settings to help you get the best shot. Here are some key options:

- **Flash**: The flash icon is located at the top of the screen, and you can toggle it between On, Off, and Auto. Flash can be useful in very low light, but iPhones are designed to perform well without it, so experiment to see when it adds value to your photos.
- **Live Photos**: Live Photos capture a short video along with the photo, giving you a moving image. You can enable or disable Live Photos by tapping the circular icon at the top of the screen. Live Photos are fun for capturing small moments with movement or sound, such as waves at the beach or laughing with friends.
- **HDR (High Dynamic Range)**: HDR enhances the brightness and detail of photos by combining multiple exposures. The HDR icon appears at the top of the screen and can be set to On, Off, or Auto. In bright or backlit scenes, HDR can help balance the lighting to capture more detail.
- **Zoom**: The iPhone 16 features high-quality zoom capabilities, allowing you to zoom in or out by pinching the screen with two fingers or using the on-screen zoom control (1x, 2x, 0.5x, etc., depending on your iPhone model). Digital zoom can affect image quality, so use it with care, especially in low-light settings.

Learning these basic adjustments gives you more control over your photos and helps you achieve specific effects.

Once you've captured some photos and videos, you can view and organize them in the Photos app. Here's how to navigate the app and manage your images:

- **Viewing Photos**: Open the Photos app, where you'll see all your images organized by **Recents** (all photos in chronological order), **Albums** (photos sorted by category), and **For You** (personalized memories and featured photos). Tap on any photo to view it in full screen, and swipe left or right to browse through your images.
- **Editing Photos**: The Photos app includes a range of basic editing tools to enhance your images. Open a photo and tap **Edit** in the top right corner. You'll see options for adjusting brightness, contrast, color saturation, and more. There are also cropping and rotating tools to help you fine-tune your images. If you're not satisfied with the edits, you can tap **Revert** to go back to the original photo.
- **Creating Albums**: Organizing your photos into albums makes it easier to find specific images later. To create a new album, go to **Albums** in the Photos app, tap the **+** icon, and select **New Album**. Give the album a name and choose the photos you want to include. This feature is helpful for sorting photos by themes, like vacations, family gatherings, or hobbies.
- **Sharing Photos**: To share photos with friends or family, tap on the photo you want to share and select the **Share** icon (a square with an arrow pointing up). You'll see options for sending the photo via **Messages**, **Mail**, or **AirDrop** (if the recipient is nearby and has an Apple device). You can also post directly to social media platforms from the Photos app.

- **Use Grid Lines**: Enabling grid lines can help you improve the composition of your photos. Go to **Settings > Camera** and turn on **Grid**. The grid divides the screen into nine sections, making it easier to follow the "rule of thirds," a technique for creating balanced compositions.

- **Hold Steady for Sharp Photos**: Blurry photos often happen due to camera shake. For sharper images, hold your iPhone with both hands and keep your elbows close to your body. In low light, you can also rest your iPhone on a stable surface or use a tripod for added stability.
- **Experiment with Angles**: Don't be afraid to try different angles when taking photos. Getting close to the ground, shooting from above, or experimenting with side angles can make your photos more dynamic and visually interesting.
- **Capture Burst Photos**: Burst mode captures a series of photos in quick succession, ideal for action shots. Simply press and hold the shutter button in Photo mode, and your iPhone will capture a sequence of images. This is especially useful for photographing moving subjects like pets or kids.

The iPhone's Camera app is a versatile tool that allows anyone to capture beautiful, high-quality photos with ease. By understanding the basics of each mode, adjusting settings to suit the situation, and experimenting with different techniques, you can take your photography to the next level. And with the Photos app, you can organize, edit, and share your images to relive and share those moments with friends and family. With a bit of practice, the Camera app will quickly become one of your favorite tools on your iPhone 16, helping you preserve memories and express creativity through photography.

Essential Apps: Notes, Calendar, and Clock

The iPhone 16 comes with several built-in apps designed to simplify your daily life. Among these, the **Notes**, **Calendar**, and **Clock** apps stand out for their practical uses, helping you stay organized, on time, and on top of ideas and reminders. Each of these apps has a variety of features that go beyond basic functionality, offering tools for organizing thoughts, scheduling events, setting alarms, and much more. This section will guide you through the essential features of each app, providing tips on how to incorporate them into your daily routines.

The Notes app on your iPhone is more than just a digital notepad. It's a versatile tool that can be used for jotting down ideas, keeping track of to-do lists, saving web links, and even storing scanned documents. Here's how to make the most of the Notes app:

- **Creating and Organizing Notes**:
  - » Open the **Notes** app and tap the **New Note** icon (a square with a pencil) to start a new note. You can begin typing immediately, add lists, and even include images or sketches.
  - » Notes are saved automatically, and you can organize them by folders. To create a folder, go to the main Notes screen, tap **New Folder** in the bottom left, name the folder, and move notes into it by tapping **Move** within each note.
  - » **Pinning Important Notes**: If you have certain notes you frequently refer to, such as a grocery list or a checklist, you

can pin them to the top of your list. Simply swipe right on the note and tap **Pin**. Pinned notes stay at the top of your list for easy access.

- **Creating Checklists and To-Do Lists**:

  » The Notes app includes a checklist feature, perfect for creating to-do lists, shopping lists, or packing lists. To create a checklist, start a new note, type your items, then select the **Checklist** icon (a checkmark in a circle) to convert each line into a checklist item.

  » As you complete tasks, you can check them off by tapping each box, helping you keep track of what's done and what still needs attention.

- **Adding Photos, Links, and Scanned Documents**:

  » In addition to text, you can insert photos, scanned documents, and links into your notes. Tap the **Camera** icon within a note to add a photo or scan a document. This feature is helpful for saving important documents, receipts, or images alongside your notes.

  » Scanned documents are saved as PDFs directly within the note, making it easy to store and access important files without needing a separate app.

- **Using Drawing and Markup Tools**:

  » If you enjoy sketching or annotating, the Notes app includes drawing tools. Tap the **Pencil** icon to access a variety of pens, markers, and colors. You can use this feature to draw diagrams, make simple sketches, or highlight text in notes. This tool is particularly useful for visually organizing information or marking up notes.

- **Locking Notes for Privacy**:

  » For sensitive information, such as passwords or personal details, you can lock individual notes. In the Notes app, swipe left on the note you want to secure, tap the **Lock** icon, and set a password or use Face ID. Once locked, the note will remain secure and hidden until unlocked with your chosen method.

The Notes app is a powerful tool for organizing your thoughts, storing information, and creating lists. Its versatility makes it an essential app for managing daily tasks and information in one accessible place.

The Calendar app is an invaluable tool for keeping track of appointments, events, birthdays, and other important dates. With a clean, easy-to-navigate interface, it allows you to organize your time efficiently and stay on top of your schedule. Here's how to get started with the Calendar app:

- **Creating Events**:

  » Open the **Calendar** app and tap the **+** icon in the top right corner to create a new event. Enter details such as the event title, location, start and end times, and a description if needed. You can also set events to repeat (daily, weekly, monthly, or yearly) for recurring appointments or reminders.

» To make sure you don't forget an event, you can add an alert that reminds you minutes, hours, or even days before the event. Setting alerts is especially useful for important dates like birthdays, anniversaries, or work meetings.

- **Viewing Your Calendar by Day, Week, and Month**:
  » The Calendar app offers several viewing options: **Day**, **Week**, and **Month**. Tap the view options at the top of the screen to switch between them.
  » The Day view displays a detailed list of events scheduled for each day, while the Week view provides a broader look at your week's activities. The Month view is ideal for identifying free days or planning longer-term events. These views help you see your schedule from different perspectives, making it easier to plan ahead.

- **Adding Multiple Calendars**:
  » You can create and manage multiple calendars in the app, each color-coded for easy identification. This is especially helpful for organizing personal events, work commitments, and family activities separately.
  » To create a new calendar, go to **Settings > Calendar > Accounts** and add accounts from email services like iCloud, Google, or Microsoft Exchange. Each account can sync with your Calendar app, making it easy to manage all events in one place.

- **Inviting Others to Events**:
  » For events involving others, such as meetings or group outings, you can send invitations directly from the Calendar app. After creating an event, scroll down to **Invitees**, enter the email addresses of the people you want to invite, and they'll receive a notification. This feature allows you to coordinate schedules with friends, family, or colleagues seamlessly.

- **Setting Up Calendar Widgets**:
  » Adding a Calendar widget to your Home Screen allows you to view upcoming events at a glance. Press and hold on the Home Screen, tap the **+** icon to open the widget gallery, and select **Calendar**. Choose the widget size that best fits your layout and add it to your Home Screen for quick access.

The Calendar app keeps you organized, reminding you of important dates and helping you manage your schedule with ease. By creating events, using multiple calendars, and setting up alerts, you'll stay on top of your commitments effortlessly.

The Clock app provides several practical features beyond just telling time. From setting alarms to managing timers and checking time zones around the world, it's a versatile app that plays a key role in managing your daily routines. Here's how to make the most of the Clock app:

- **Setting Alarms**:
  » Open the **Clock** app and go to the **Alarm** tab. Tap the **+** icon to set a new alarm, choosing the time, repeat schedule,

sound, and label for each alarm. You can set alarms to repeat on specific days, making it easy to set up regular wake-up calls or reminders.

» Alarms can be customized with different sounds, so you can select a tone that's gentle or loud, depending on your preferences. You can also add labels to alarms, such as "Morning Medication" or "Exercise Reminder," for added convenience.

- **Using the Timer**:
  » The **Timer** tab is useful for counting down activities, such as cooking, workouts, or timed tasks. Open the Timer tab, set the desired duration, and tap **Start**. You'll hear an alert when the timer reaches zero.
  » You can choose different sounds for your timers, allowing you to select a distinct alert for each activity. Timer alerts ensure that you stay on schedule for short-term tasks.

- **Using the Stopwatch**:
  » The **Stopwatch** tab is helpful for timing activities like exercise or tracking the length of calls or meetings. Tap **Start** to begin timing, and **Stop** to end. You can also use the **Lap** function to mark specific intervals, which is useful for tracking progress in activities that involve multiple rounds or stages.

- **World Clock**:
  » If you frequently communicate with people in different time zones, the **World Clock** tab is an invaluable tool. Open the World Clock tab and tap the **+** icon to add different cities or time zones. This lets you quickly check the time in other locations, making it easier to schedule calls or meetings across time zones.

- **Bedtime Feature**:
  » The **Bedtime** feature (found within the Alarm tab) helps you establish a consistent sleep schedule. Set your ideal wake-up time, and the Bedtime feature will suggest a bedtime based on the amount of sleep you want. You can enable **Bedtime Reminders** to receive alerts when it's time to wind down for the night, promoting a healthy sleep routine.

The Clock app's versatile features make it an essential tool for managing daily routines, from waking up on time to tracking tasks and staying connected across time zones.

With the Notes, Calendar, and Clock apps, your iPhone 16 becomes an invaluable assistant for staying organized, managing your schedule, and maintaining productivity. These apps provide simple yet powerful tools to keep track of tasks, events, and reminders, allowing you to stay on top of your commitments and make the most of each day. By exploring the unique features of each app, you'll be able to integrate them seamlessly into your life, enhancing your daily routines with ease and efficiency.

Setting Up Reminders and Tasks

The Reminders app on your iPhone 16 is a powerful tool for managing tasks, organizing to-do lists, and ensuring nothing falls through the cracks. Whether you need to remember to pick up groceries, schedule a doctor's appointment, or set a recurring reminder for a weekly meeting, the Reminders app makes it easy to stay on track. In this section, we'll walk through the essentials of setting up reminders and tasks, using advanced features like priority settings, tags, and location-based alerts, and creating lists that help you organize every area of your life.

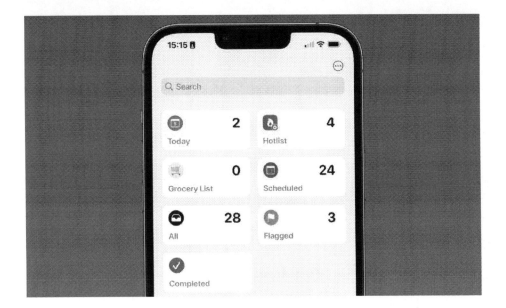

The Reminders app is designed to be straightforward and user-friendly. Here's how to get started:

- **Opening the Reminders App**: The Reminders app comes pre-installed on your iPhone, so you can simply open it from your Home Screen or App Library. When you open the app, you'll see options to create new reminders and organize them into lists.
- **Understanding the Layout**: The main screen of the Reminders app displays all your existing lists (like "Today," "Scheduled," "Flagged," and "All"). You'll also see any custom lists you've created, allowing you to organize reminders by categories or themes. Tap any list to view and manage the reminders within it.

Adding a reminder is quick and easy. Here's how to create your first reminder:

- **Adding a Reminder**:
  » Tap **New Reminder** at the bottom of the screen, type in a description of your task (e.g., "Buy groceries" or "Call Mom"), and hit **Done** to save. This basic reminder will appear under your default list, usually "Today" or "Scheduled."
- **Setting Due Dates and Times**:
  » To set a specific due date and time, tap the reminder after you create it, then tap the **calendar** and **clock** icons to set when you want to be reminded. You can choose exact dates and times, ensuring that your reminders pop up exactly when needed.

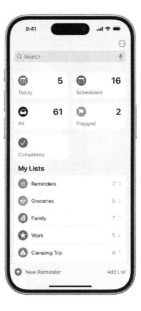

To make reminders even more effective, the Reminders app includes several advanced features. Here's how to use them:

- **Adding Priority Levels**:
  - » Each reminder can be assigned a priority level (low, medium, or high) to help you distinguish between urgent tasks and those that can wait. To set a priority, tap the reminder, select **Details**, and choose your desired priority level. High-priority reminders will stand out, making it easier to identify essential tasks at a glance.

- **Creating Recurring Reminders**:
  - » For tasks that need to be completed regularly, like "Take medication" or "Pay bills," you can create recurring reminders. Tap the reminder, select **Details**, and choose **Repeat**. You can set the frequency (daily, weekly, monthly, or custom intervals), ensuring that recurring tasks appear automatically without needing to re-enter them.

- **Location-Based Reminders**:
  - » One of the most useful features of the Reminders app is the ability to create location-based reminders. This feature triggers a reminder when you arrive at or leave a specific location. For example, you could set a reminder to "Buy milk" when you arrive at the grocery store.
  - » To set a location-based reminder, tap on the reminder, go to **Details**, and select **When I Arrive** or **When I Leave** under the Location section. Enter the location you'd like to associate with the reminder, and your iPhone will notify you accordingly.

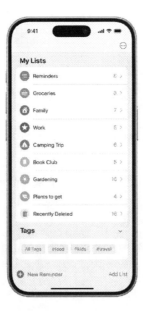

The Reminders app allows you to create custom lists to keep related tasks organized. Lists make it easy to manage multiple tasks in different areas of life, like "Work," "Personal," "Shopping," or "Projects." Here's how to set up and organize lists:

- **Creating a Custom List**:
  - » Go to the main screen in the Reminders app and tap **Add List** at the bottom. Choose a name for the list, select a color, and, if desired, an icon that represents the list's theme. Once created, your custom list will appear on the main screen, allowing you to add related tasks directly to it.

- **Using Tags for Better Organization**:
  - » Tags are a recent addition to the Reminders app that allow you to add keywords to reminders, which makes it easy to categorize and filter tasks across different lists. For example, you could tag reminders with keywords like "Urgent," "Errand," or "Family." To add a tag, simply type **#tagname** within the reminder or in the Tags section of the reminder's details.
  - » Once you've added tags, you can tap on a tag in the main Reminders screen to view all reminders associated with that tag, regardless of which list they're in. This feature is particularly helpful for keeping track of tasks by theme or priority.

Smart Lists are custom lists that automatically organize reminders based on specific criteria, like due dates, priority, tags, or location. Here's how to make the most of Smart Lists:

- **Creating a Smart List**:
  - » Tap **Add List** and select **Make into Smart List**. Then choose the criteria for the list, such as reminders with the "High Priority" tag or those due within the next three days. Your iPhone will automatically add reminders to the Smart List based on these criteria.

- **Examples of Smart Lists**:
  - » **High Priority**: Track only high-priority tasks by setting up a Smart List that includes reminders with the "High" priority level.
  - » **Upcoming Tasks**: Create a Smart List for reminders due within the next week to give yourself an overview of what's coming up soon.
  - » **Location-Based Tasks**: If you frequently create location-based reminders, you could set up a Smart List to track tasks associated with specific locations, like errands or shopping lists.

Smart Lists provide a convenient way to automate organization and access reminders quickly based on urgency, location, or timing.

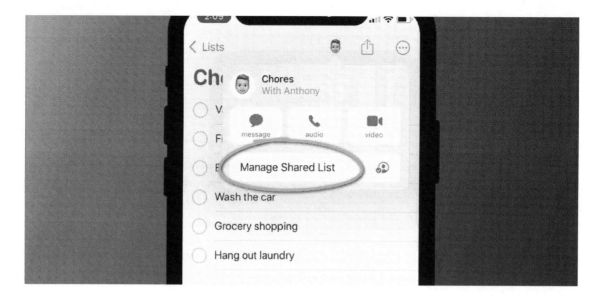

Once you've created reminders, it's essential to review and manage them effectively to stay organized. Here are some helpful tips:

- **Marking Reminders as Complete**:
  - » When you complete a task, simply tap the empty circle next to the reminder to mark it as done. Completed reminders disappear from active lists, but you can view them later by tapping on **Show Completed** in each list.

- **Reordering and Sorting**:
  - » If you want to prioritize tasks within a list, you can reorder reminders by pressing and holding a reminder, then dragging it to your preferred position. In the **Details** section of each list, you'll also find sorting options that let you organize reminders by due date, priority, or creation date.

- **Editing Reminders**:
  - » To edit a reminder, tap on it to open the details and make any necessary adjustments, like changing the due date, time, priority, or location. Regularly updating reminders keeps them relevant and ensures you're notified at the right times.

Siri can quickly create reminders hands-free, making it easier to add tasks without opening the Reminders app. Here's how to use Siri to add reminders:

- **Creating a Reminder with Siri**:
  - » Say, "Hey Siri, remind me to [task] at [time or location]." For example, you could say, "Hey Siri, remind me to call the

dentist at 3 PM" or "Hey Siri, remind me to pick up dry cleaning when I leave work." Siri will add the reminder automatically, complete with the specified time or location.

Checking Your Reminders with Siri:

» You can also use Siri to check your reminders by saying, "Hey Siri, what are my reminders for today?" or "Hey Siri, do I have any reminders for this week?" Siri will provide a list of upcoming reminders based on your request.

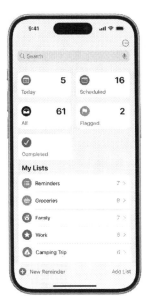

Here are a few additional tips to help you make the most of the Reminders app:

- **Set Clear, Specific Reminders**: To stay organized, write reminders that are clear and specific. Instead of a vague reminder like "Call," write "Call Dr. Smith to schedule appointment." This specificity saves time and ensures you know exactly what action to take.
- **Regularly Review Your Lists**: Take a few minutes each day or week to review your lists and check off completed tasks. Updating and reviewing your reminders regularly ensures you're staying on top of all tasks.
- **Use Notifications Wisely**: Too many notifications can be overwhelming, so focus on setting alerts only for critical reminders. For lower-priority tasks, you can add them to lists without setting specific alerts, reducing unnecessary notifications.

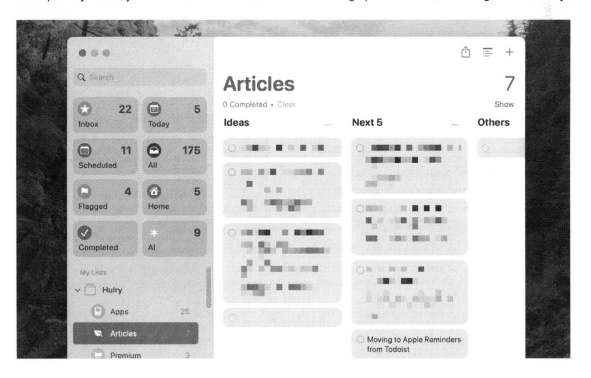

The Reminders app can integrate with other apps and devices for seamless task management:

- **Syncing Across Devices**: Reminders created on your iPhone will sync automatically across all Apple devices signed in with the same Apple ID, ensuring that you have access to your to-do lists whether you're on your iPhone, iPad, or Mac.
- **Integrating with Calendar**: You can view your reminders in the Calendar app if they're scheduled with a date and time. This integration helps you see tasks alongside appointments, making it easier to manage both schedules and to-dos.
- **Using Reminders with CarPlay**: If you have CarPlay in your vehicle, you can add and check reminders while driving using Siri, helping you stay organized on the go.

With these features, the Reminders app transforms your iPhone into a powerful organizational tool, making it easy to manage tasks, stay on schedule, and never miss a reminder. By creating clear reminders, organizing them with lists and tags, and using advanced features like location-based alerts, you'll be able to keep track of all your important tasks and responsibilities.

CHAPTER 5
STAYING CONNECTED

Welcome to Chapter 5: Staying Connected! In today's digital world, staying in touch with family, friends, and colleagues has never been easier. Your iPhone 16 is equipped with a range of tools and apps that make communication simple, whether through texting, sharing photos, sending emails, or connecting on social media. This chapter will guide you through the essential functions that help you stay connected with the people who matter most to you.

We'll start by covering the basics of **sending texts, photos, and video messages**. The Messages app on your iPhone allows you to send instant messages, photos, videos, and even voice recordings, keeping conversations engaging and personal. Texting is a quick and efficient way to stay in touch, whether you're sending a quick update, sharing photos with loved ones, or using FaceTime for live video chats. We'll guide you through the steps to send different types of messages, manage your conversations, and even add fun touches like emojis, GIFs, and stickers to make your messages more interactive.

Next, we'll dive into the **basics of social media**, specifically focusing on Facebook and Messenger. Social media is a fantastic way to keep up with family and friends, share photos and life updates, and join groups of people with similar interests. If you're new to social media or haven't used it much, we'll introduce you to Facebook, one of the most popular platforms. You'll learn how to set up an account, navigate your news feed, post updates, and use Messenger to communicate directly with friends. Social media can be a great tool for staying in touch, and this section will help you use it confidently and safely.

Finally, we'll go over **email setup and management**, which is essential for handling communication that's a bit more formal or long-form, like messages from family, news updates, or appointment reminders. Your iPhone's Mail app makes it easy to access your email accounts in one place, whether you use Gmail, Yahoo, iCloud, or another provider. In this section, we'll cover how to set up your email, manage your inbox, and organize messages, so you can keep track of important emails without feeling overwhelmed. We'll also provide tips on how to identify and avoid spam emails, keeping your inbox safe and secure.

Staying connected is more than just sending a text or making a call—it's about maintaining relationships, staying informed, and sharing moments in meaningful ways. By the end of this chapter, you'll be familiar with the tools and techniques that make staying in touch easier and more enjoyable, from texting and social media to managing emails efficiently. Let's get started and make sure your iPhone is fully set up to help you stay connected with those who matter most, no matter where you are!

Sending Texts, Photos, and Video Messages

The Messages app on your iPhone 16 is a powerful tool for staying connected, offering features that go far beyond basic texting. You can use it to send texts, photos, videos, voice messages, and more, making communication engaging and versatile. Whether you're sharing a quick message, sending photos from a recent family event, or recording a video message, the Messages app keeps you in touch in meaningful ways. This section will walk you through the basics of using the Messages app, adding multimedia to your conversations, and customizing your messaging experience.

The Messages app is Apple's built-in messaging platform, allowing you to send both SMS (regular text messages) and iMessages (Apple's enhanced messaging service) in one place. Here's how to get started:

- **Opening the Messages App**: To open the Messages app, tap the green icon with a white speech bubble on your Home Screen or in your App Library.
- **Understanding SMS vs. iMessage**: The Messages app automatically detects if you're messaging another Apple device. If so, it uses iMessage, indicated by blue text bubbles. Messages to non-Apple devices appear as green text bubbles, which means they're sent as SMS and may incur charges depending on your phone plan.
- **Starting a New Conversation**: Tap the **Compose** icon (a square with a pencil) in the top-right corner to start a new conversation. Enter the contact's name or phone number, type your message, and tap **Send** to deliver it.

Text messages are a quick and simple way to communicate, perfect for brief updates or staying in touch throughout the day. Here are some tips to make the most of your text messages:

- **Typing and Sending Messages**: Start typing in the text field at the bottom of the screen, then tap the **Send** button to send your message.
- **Adding Emojis and GIFs**: The Messages app includes a built-in emoji keyboard, which you can access by tapping the **smiley face** icon on your keyboard. Emojis add a personal touch to your messages and make them more expressive. You can also add animated **GIFs** by tapping the **App Store** icon next to the text field, selecting **#images**, and searching for a GIF to match your message's tone.
- **Using Quick Reactions**: iMessage offers quick reactions, known as **Tapbacks**, that let you respond to a message with

a simple icon, like a thumbs-up or heart. To use Tapbacks, press and hold the message you received, then select the reaction you'd like to send. It's a fast way to acknowledge messages without typing.

View contact info and conversation details.

Share photos, audio messages, your location, stickers, and more.

Photos and videos make messaging more dynamic and allow you to share moments visually. The Messages app makes it easy to send both, whether you're sharing a quick snapshot or a longer video clip.

- **Sending a Photo**:
  - » Tap the **Photos** icon next to the text field to access your photo library. Select the photo you want to send, add an optional caption, and tap **Send** to deliver it.
  - » You can also take a new photo directly within the Messages app. Tap the **Camera** icon, snap your photo, then tap **Send**. This feature is useful if you want to capture and share a moment instantly.

- **Sending a Video**:
  - » To send a video from your library, tap the **Photos** icon, then select a video. If you're recording a video directly in Messages, tap the **Camera** icon, switch to Video mode, and hold the **Record** button. Once you're done recording, tap **Send**.
  - » Keep in mind that large video files may take longer to send, especially if you're not connected to Wi-Fi. For very large videos, you can send a shortened version by trimming the clip in the Photos app before sharing.

iMessage offers a variety of effects and enhancements to make your messages more engaging. Here are some fun options to explore:

- **Bubble Effects**:
  - » Bubble effects apply special animations to individual messages. After typing a message, press and hold the **Send** button, then choose **Bubble** effects like **Slam** (which makes the message appear forcefully), **Loud** (which enlarges the text), or **Invisible Ink** (which hides the message until tapped).
  - » Bubble effects are a playful way to emphasize certain messages, especially in casual conversations with family or friends.

- **Screen Effects**:
  - » Screen effects animate the entire screen when you send a message, creating a more immersive experience. After typing a message, press and hold the Send button, then select **Screen**. You'll see effects like **Balloons**, **Confetti**, **Lasers**, and **Fireworks**.
  - » Screen effects are perfect for celebrations or moments when you want to make a big impact with your message.

- **Digital Touch and Handwriting**:
  - » **Digital Touch** lets you send drawings, taps, or heartbeats in messages. To access it, tap the **App Store** icon and select the **heart icon**. You can draw shapes, tap the screen to create taps, or press with two fingers to send a heartbeat. Digital Touch messages add a personal touch to conversations.
  - » You can also send handwritten messages by turning your phone sideways (landscape mode) in the Messages app, where you'll see a blank screen to write or draw with your finger. This feature is ideal for sending quick, personalized notes.

Sometimes, a voice message conveys emotion and tone better than text alone. The Messages app makes it easy to send quick audio messages:

- **Recording and Sending Audio**:
  - » To send an audio message, press and hold the **Microphone** icon next to the text field. Start speaking, then release the icon to send the recording. If you want to cancel the message, swipe left before releasing.
  - » Audio messages are useful for sending detailed information or just saying hello when you're on the go. Unlike text, audio captures the nuances of your voice, making your message feel more personal.

- **Setting Audio Message Expiration**:
  - » By default, audio messages expire after two minutes to save storage space. If you want to keep audio messages permanently, go to **Settings > Messages** and select **Expire > Never** under **Audio Messages**. This ensures you can access old audio messages whenever you want.

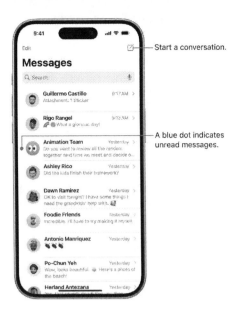

With iMessage, you can keep conversations organized and easily access old messages. Here are a few tips for managing your message threads:

- **Pinning Conversations**:
  - » If you frequently message certain people, you can pin their conversations to the top of your Messages app. To pin a conversation, swipe right on it and tap **Pin**. Pinned conversations stay at the top, making it easy to access them quickly.
- **Muting Conversations**:
  - » To avoid notifications from a busy group chat or conversation, you can mute it. Open the conversation, tap the **Contact's Name** at the top, and toggle on **Hide Alerts**. You'll still receive messages, but without the constant notifications.
- **Deleting Messages**:
  - » To delete individual messages, press and hold the message, then select **More** and choose the messages you'd like to delete. For entire conversations, swipe left on the conversation from the main screen and tap **Delete**. Keep in mind that deleting messages on your end doesn't remove them from the recipient's device.

Group messages allow you to communicate with multiple people at once, ideal for planning events or keeping in touch with family. Here's how to create and manage group messages:

- **Creating a Group Message**:

- » To start a group message, tap the **Compose** icon and add multiple contacts in the "To" field. Once you've added everyone, type your message and hit **Send**.

- • **Naming and Customizing Group Chats**:

  - » For easy identification, you can name your group conversation. Open the group chat, tap the group photo or contact bubbles at the top, then tap **Change Name and Photo**. You can choose a custom name and set a group icon.

- • **Managing Group Notifications**:

  - » In busy group chats, you may want to mute notifications or only receive alerts when mentioned by name. Open the group chat, tap the group details at the top, and toggle **Hide Alerts**. To receive specific notifications when mentioned, simply type @ followed by a person's name to tag them in the conversation.

With FaceTime integration, you can start a video call directly from the Messages app, allowing you to switch from texting to live conversation effortlessly:

- • **Starting a FaceTime Call**:

  - » Open a conversation in Messages, tap the **Contact's Name** at the top, then select **FaceTime**. This will start a FaceTime video call if both you and the recipient have FaceTime enabled.

The Messages app on your iPhone 16 is a robust platform for staying connected in meaningful ways. From simple text messages to multimedia sharing and engaging effects, it offers a versatile set of tools that keep conversations lively and personal. By using these features to communicate, you'll find that staying in touch with family and friends has never been more enjoyable or interactive. Whether you're sending a quick update, sharing photos and videos, or adding fun animations, the Messages app lets you express yourself and connect with others in ways that go beyond just words.

Basics of Social Media (Facebook, Messenger)

Social media has become a central part of staying connected with family, friends, and communities, and Facebook is one of the most popular platforms for doing just that. Facebook allows you to share photos, videos, updates, and even join interest-based groups, while its Messenger app provides a dedicated space for instant messaging. Whether you're new to social media or want a refresher on Facebook's main features, this section will guide you through setting up a Facebook account, navigating the platform, sharing posts, and using Messenger to communicate directly with friends.

Facebook serves as a platform where you can connect with people, share life updates, and join communities with shared interests. Here's how to set up an account and start using Facebook:

* **Creating an Account**:
  * » If you haven't created an account yet, download the **Facebook** app from the App Store, open it, and tap **Create New Account**. You'll be prompted to enter basic details, including your name, email or phone number, password, and date of birth. Follow the on-screen instructions to complete your registration.
  * » Facebook may ask for some additional information, like a profile picture and a few personal details, to help others recognize you. Adding a profile picture and cover photo (a larger photo at the top of your profile) is optional but helps personalize your account.

* **Setting Up Your Profile**:
  * » Once you've created your account, tap on your profile picture in the upper left corner of the Facebook app to view and edit your profile. Here, you can add more personal details like where you live, your work history, and education. Completing your profile helps others identify and connect with you.
  * » Privacy is important on Facebook, so you can adjust who can see your personal information by going to **Settings > Privacy**. This allows you to control which parts of your profile are visible to friends, friends of friends, or the public.

The home screen is the main area where you'll find your News Feed, a continuous scroll of posts shared by your friends and pages you follow. Here's how to navigate and make the most of it:

* **News Feed**:

» Your News Feed displays recent posts, including updates, photos, and videos shared by your friends, groups, and pages. You can scroll through to see what's new in your network.

» Each post shows who shared it, the date and time, and may include options to **Like**, **Comment**, and **Share**. Liking or commenting on posts is a simple way to interact with others and show appreciation for what they share.

- **Search Bar**:

» The search bar at the top of the screen lets you quickly find friends, pages, groups, and topics of interest. Simply type in a name, keyword, or phrase, and Facebook will display relevant results. This is helpful for reconnecting with friends, discovering new content, or joining interest-based groups.

- **Notifications and Friend Requests**:

» Notifications (the bell icon) alert you to activity involving you, such as comments on your posts, likes, or friend requests. Tap the notification to view details and respond if needed.

» The friend request icon shows pending requests from people who want to connect with you. You can accept or decline requests based on your preferences.

- **Groups and Pages**:

» Facebook lets you join **Groups** and **Pages** based on interests, hobbies, or communities. Groups are spaces where people with shared interests can post content, ask questions, and participate in discussions. Pages, on the other hand, are typically created by businesses, organizations, or public figures.

» To join a group or follow a page, use the search bar to find topics you're interested in and select **Join** or **Follow**. You'll see updates from groups and pages in your News Feed.

One of the core features of Facebook is sharing your own content, allowing you to keep friends updated on your life or express your thoughts. Here's how to create posts:

- **Creating a Post**:

» From the home screen, tap the **What's on your mind?** box at the top to create a post. You can write a message, add a photo, tag friends, and even include a location if you're somewhere special.

» Before posting, you can choose who will see it by tapping **Audience Selector** (e.g., Friends, Public, or Only Me). This allows you to control the visibility of each post, making it easy to share personal updates with only specific people if you prefer.

- **Sharing Photos and Videos**:

» To share a photo or video, tap **Photo/Video** under the post box, select an image or video from your gallery, and add a caption if you'd like. Facebook supports multiple photos and videos in a single post, making it easy to share memories from an event or trip.

» You can also go live by selecting **Live Video**, which broadcasts in real-time to your Facebook friends or followers. Live videos are great for special events, like family gatherings or travel experiences, where you want others to join in as they happen.

• **Using Stories**:

» Facebook Stories allow you to share photos and short videos that disappear after 24 hours, similar to Instagram Stories. Tap on **Your Story** at the top of the home screen to add a quick update, which appears only for a limited time. Stories are perfect for sharing spontaneous moments or quick updates without keeping them on your profile permanently.

Facebook Messenger is a separate app that's directly linked to Facebook, allowing you to have private conversations with friends. Here's how to set up and use Messenger:

• **Downloading and Setting Up Messenger**:

» Download the **Messenger** app from the App Store and log in with your Facebook credentials. Once logged in, you'll see a list of your Facebook friends, making it easy to start a chat.

» You can send text messages, photos, videos, and even audio messages. Messenger's interface is similar to texting apps, with a familiar layout that makes chatting simple.

• **Starting a Conversation**:

» To start a new chat, tap the **Compose** icon in the top right corner, select a friend, and begin typing. Tap **Send** to deliver your message.

» Messenger also supports group chats. To start a group conversation, select multiple friends, type your message, and send it. Group chats are great for planning events or keeping in touch with multiple family members or friends.

• **Sending Photos, Videos, and Voice Messages**:

» Messenger lets you share multimedia easily. Tap the **Camera** icon to take a photo or record a video directly in the app, or select the **Photos** icon to choose from your gallery.

» To send a voice message, press and hold the **Microphone** icon, record your message, and release it to send. Voice messages are a personal way to stay in touch and are useful when you have a longer message or want to add a personal touch.

• **Using Reactions and Stickers**:

» Like on Facebook, Messenger allows you to use reactions (thumbs-up, heart, etc.) on individual messages. Press and hold the message to see the reaction options, and tap to select one.

» Messenger also includes a library of stickers and GIFs that you can add to your conversations, making your chats more fun and expressive.

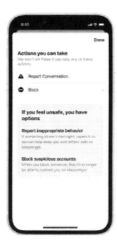

It's essential to be mindful of your privacy and security on Facebook and Messenger. Here are some tips for staying safe:

- **Adjusting Privacy Settings**:
  - » Go to **Settings > Privacy** on Facebook to adjust who can see your posts, send you friend requests, or view your profile information. You can customize each setting to control your visibility on the platform.

- **Blocking Unwanted Contacts**:
  - » If you receive unwanted messages or friend requests, you can block the person by going to their profile and selecting **Block**. This removes their ability to interact with you on Facebook and Messenger.

- **Recognizing and Avoiding Scams**:
  - » Be cautious of messages from people you don't know, especially if they ask for personal information or money. Scammers sometimes pose as friends or trusted individuals, so it's best to confirm the person's identity before engaging in suspicious conversations.

Engagement on social media can be enjoyable and rewarding when done responsibly. By using features like liking, commenting, and sharing thoughtfully, you can maintain positive interactions with your friends and communities.

Facebook and Messenger offer versatile ways to connect, communicate, and share, making it easy to stay engaged with people in your life. From sharing photos and updates on Facebook to chatting directly in Messenger, these apps provide a comprehensive social experience, all while giving you control over your privacy and visibility. Once you're comfortable navigating these tools, you'll find social media a valuable resource for staying connected, sharing moments, and fostering relationships online.

Email Setup and Management

Email is an essential tool for staying connected, receiving important updates, and managing day-to-day communication. Your iPhone 16's Mail app makes it easy to set up, organize, and manage multiple email accounts in one place, so you can access all your messages conveniently. Whether you're setting up a new email account or looking for ways to organize your inbox, this section will guide you through the essentials of email setup and management on your iPhone.

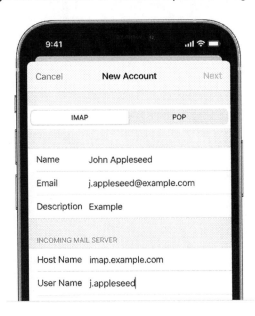

The Mail app supports a wide range of email providers, including Gmail, Yahoo, Outlook, iCloud, and others. Here's how to add an email account and get started with the Mail app:

- **Adding a New Email Account**:
  - » Open **Settings** on your iPhone, scroll down, and select **Mail**. Tap **Accounts** and then **Add Account**.
  - » You'll see a list of popular email providers. Select your email provider (e.g., Gmail, Yahoo, or Outlook). If you don't see your provider listed, choose **Other** to enter your email details manually.
  - » Enter your email address and password, and follow the on-screen instructions to complete the setup. Once you're signed in, your iPhone will automatically sync your email, contacts, and calendar (if applicable) with the Mail app.
- **Setting Up Multiple Email Accounts**:
  - » If you have more than one email account, you can add each account separately by repeating the above steps. The Mail app will organize messages by account, allowing you to view all emails in a unified inbox or check each account individually.
  - » Once your accounts are set up, you can choose which accounts you want to receive email notifications for, helping you prioritize the accounts that matter most.

The Mail app's layout is simple and intuitive, making it easy to access and manage emails. Here's a quick overview of its main sections:

- **Mailboxes**: When you open the Mail app, you'll see a list of your **Mailboxes** on the main screen. Mailboxes include your **Inbox**, **Sent**, **Trash**, **Drafts**, and any custom folders or filters.
    - » **All Inboxes** displays emails from all accounts in one place, while individual inboxes allow you to view emails from specific accounts.
- **Inbox**: The Inbox is where all new emails arrive. You can tap on any email to open it, read its contents, and respond if needed. Emails are typically sorted by date, with the most recent at the top.
- **Search Bar**: The search bar at the top of the screen allows you to quickly find specific emails by entering keywords, sender names, or subject lines. This feature is particularly useful when you need to locate older emails or specific information in a large inbox.

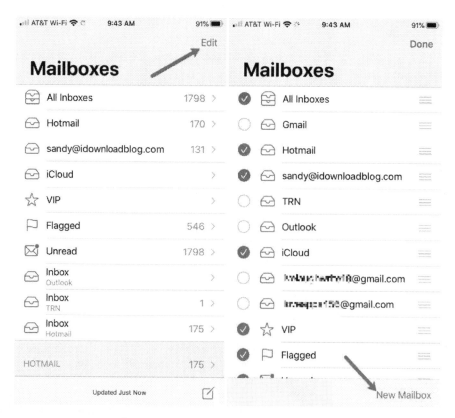

As your inbox grows, organizing emails into folders and using filters can help you keep track of important messages and reduce clutter:

- **Creating Folders**:
  - » To create folders, go to the Mail app's main screen, select your email account, and tap **Edit** in the upper right corner. Then select **New Mailbox** and give it a name (e.g., "Work," "Family," "Receipts"). You can move emails into these folders to keep your inbox organized by category.
  - » Once created, folders appear under the selected email account, and you can move emails to them by swiping left on an email, tapping **More**, and choosing **Move to Folder**.

- **Using VIP Senders**:
  - » The VIP feature allows you to designate certain contacts as VIPs, whose emails will always appear in a special VIP mailbox. To add a contact as VIP, open an email from them, tap their name, and select **Add to VIP**.
  - » VIPs make it easy to find important emails from family, close friends, or important contacts without searching through your entire inbox.

- **Applying Filters**:
  - » Filters in the Mail app help you display only specific types of emails, such as unread emails, flagged messages, or emails with attachments. Tap the **Filter** icon at the bottom left of the inbox and select a filter option. This allows you to focus on important messages or quickly find emails that meet certain criteria.

The Mail app provides several options for managing emails, from replying and forwarding to archiving and deleting. Here's how to make the most of these functions:

- **Reading and Replying to Emails**:
  - » To open an email, simply tap on it. Once open, you'll see options at the bottom of the screen to **Reply**, **Reply All**, or **Forward**. Replying allows you to respond directly to the sender, while forwarding lets you share the email with others.
  - » If you need to add an attachment, tap **Attach File** in the reply options to include a document or photo.

- **Flagging Important Emails**:
  - » If an email requires follow-up or is particularly important, you can flag it by swiping left on the email and tapping **Flag**. This adds a small flag icon to the email, making it easy to find in the future.
  - » You can view all flagged emails by selecting the **Flagged** mailbox, which collects flagged emails from all accounts.

- **Deleting and Archiving Emails**:
  - » To delete an email, swipe left on it and tap **Delete**. Deleted emails are moved to the **Trash** folder, where they remain temporarily before being permanently deleted.
  - » If you prefer to archive emails instead of deleting them, swipe left and select **Archive**. Archived emails are removed from the inbox but saved in the **All Mail** folder, where you can access them later if needed.

- **Marking Emails as Read or Unread**:
  - » If you want to mark an email as read or unread, swipe left on it, tap **More**, and select the relevant option. Marking an email as unread can serve as a visual reminder to revisit it later.

Creating new emails is simple in the Mail app, and you have several options for formatting and attachments:

- **Starting a New Email**:
  - » Tap the **Compose** icon in the bottom right corner to start a new email. In the **To** field, enter the recipient's email address. You can add multiple recipients or use the **Cc** (carbon copy) or **Bcc** (blind carbon copy) fields as needed.
  - » Add a subject in the **Subject** field to let recipients know what the email is about, then type your message in the body.

- **Adding Attachments and Photos**:
  - » To attach a document, tap within the message body, then select **Attach File** or **Insert Photo or Video**. You can attach documents from iCloud Drive, your Files app, or your Photos library, making it easy to include relevant files with your message.

- **Using Rich Text Formatting**:
  - » The Mail app allows you to use rich text formatting for your emails, enabling you to add bold, italic, or underlined text. Select the text you want to format, tap **Aa**, and choose the desired style. This feature is especially useful when emphasizing important points.

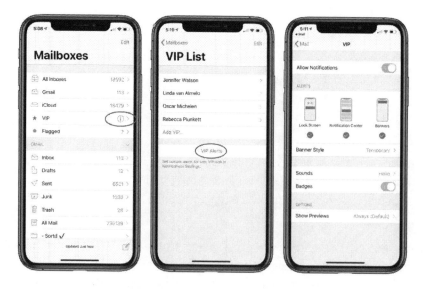

Email notifications help you stay updated on new messages, but you can customize them to suit your needs and avoid unnecessary interruptions:

- **Setting Up Notifications by Account**:
  - » To receive notifications only from specific accounts, go to **Settings > Notifications > Mail**, select each email account, and customize alert settings. You can choose from options like sounds, banners, and badges, ensuring you're notified of emails that matter.

- **Enabling VIP Notifications**:
  - » If you've set up VIP contacts, you can enable notifications specifically for VIP emails by going to **Settings > Notifications > Mail** and selecting **VIP**. This ensures that emails from important contacts receive special alerts.

The Mail app offers a few additional tools to enhance your email experience, especially for frequent users:

- **Scheduling Emails to Send Later**:
  - » Though not built into the native Mail app, some third-party email apps (like Spark or Outlook) allow you to schedule emails to be sent at a specific time. This is useful for sending emails at optimal times or ensuring you don't forget to send them later.

- **Using Mail Drop for Large Attachments**:
  - » If you're sending large files, iCloud's **Mail Drop** feature allows you to attach files up to 5GB in size. Instead of attaching the file directly, Mail Drop creates a download link that the recipient can access. Mail Drop activates automatically when you attach large files in an iCloud email.

- **Organizing with Smart Mailboxes**:
  - » Smart Mailboxes allow you to create custom views that filter emails based on certain criteria, such as unread messages or emails with attachments. To set up a Smart Mailbox, go to **Mailboxes**, tap **Edit**, and select the Smart Mailbox options that meet your needs.

**Personalized suggestions
help keep your inbox clean**

Managing your inbox effectively helps you maintain order and security:

- **Unsubscribing from Unwanted Newsletters**:
  - » If you receive newsletters you no longer want, open the email and look for an **Unsubscribe** link, typically found at the bottom. This will reduce inbox clutter and ensure you only receive relevant messages.

- **Recognizing and Avoiding Spam**:
  - » Be cautious of emails from unknown senders or with suspicious links. Common signs of spam include requests for personal information or offers that seem too good to be true. Use the **Mark as Junk** option to flag spam emails, helping prevent future unwanted messages.

The Mail app on your iPhone 16 offers a complete toolkit for managing email efficiently. From setting up accounts to organizing your inbox and using notifications selectively, these features make it easy to handle communication effectively. By taking advantage of the organizational and security tools, you can keep your inbox clean, organized, and focused on messages that matter.

CHAPTER 6
ONLINE SAFETY

Welcome to Chapter 6: Online Safety! As our lives become increasingly connected through the internet, ensuring a safe online experience has never been more important. The internet provides us with convenient ways to stay informed, shop, connect with others, and manage daily tasks, but it also comes with risks. This chapter focuses on practical steps you can take to protect yourself and your personal information while browsing, using apps, and interacting online.

We'll start by discussing **safe browsing practices** with Safari, Apple's built-in web browser. Safari includes several features designed to make your browsing experience secure, such as blocking malicious sites, managing cookies, and offering a private browsing mode. You'll learn how to identify secure websites, avoid risky links, and clear your browsing history to protect your privacy.

Next, we'll cover **recognizing scams and avoiding spam**, which are essential skills for safe internet use. Scams often appear as emails, texts, or even pop-ups on websites, attempting to trick you into revealing personal information or making payments. We'll explore the most common types of scams, including phishing emails, fake calls, and fraudulent links, and give you tips on spotting suspicious content. Additionally, you'll learn how to reduce spam in your inbox and manage settings to prevent unwanted messages.

Finally, we'll delve into **managing privacy and app permissions**. Apps often request permission to access your location, photos, contacts, and other data, and it's important to review these requests carefully. The iPhone provides tools to control what data each app can access, giving you greater control over your privacy. We'll walk you through adjusting these settings, as well as tips for reviewing app permissions regularly and ensuring that your personal information is only accessible to trusted apps.

In today's digital world, protecting your information and knowing how to identify threats are essential skills. By following the guidance in this chapter, you'll be able to navigate the internet with greater confidence, keeping your data safe and avoiding common online pitfalls. Let's dive in and make sure your online experience is both enjoyable and secure, empowering you to make the most of your iPhone and the internet.

Safe Browsing with Safari

Browsing the internet is one of the primary uses of a smartphone, and Apple's Safari browser on the iPhone 16 is designed with built-in features to make your experience both secure and enjoyable. While the internet provides access to a wealth of information and resources, it's essential to use caution to protect your privacy and avoid potential risks. This section will guide you through Safari's safe browsing features, covering how to identify secure sites, manage settings for optimal security, use private browsing, and protect yourself from online threats.

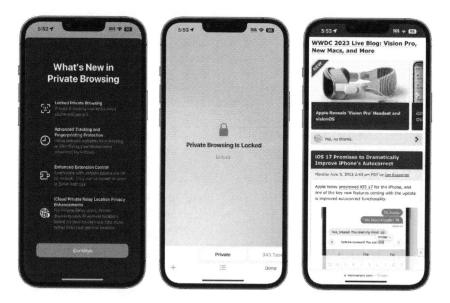

Safari includes several features designed to enhance your security while browsing:

- **Fraudulent Website Warning**: Safari alerts you when you attempt to visit a site that is potentially fraudulent or unsafe. This feature, known as the **Fraudulent Website Warning**, is enabled by default and helps protect you from phishing sites—websites that mimic legitimate ones to trick you into revealing personal information.
- **Intelligent Tracking Prevention**: Safari's Intelligent Tracking Prevention (ITP) feature blocks third-party tracking cookies, which are often used to monitor your online activity across multiple websites. ITP reduces the ability of advertisers and other entities to track your browsing habits, helping to protect your privacy.
- **Pop-Up Blocker**: Safari's built-in pop-up blocker prevents unwanted pop-ups from appearing while you're browsing. Pop-ups can sometimes contain malicious content or lead to deceptive sites, so keeping this feature enabled is an important step in safe browsing.

To ensure these features are activated, go to **Settings > Safari** and verify that **Fraudulent Website Warning**, **Block Pop-ups**, and **Prevent Cross-Site Tracking** are all enabled.

When visiting websites, it's important to recognize signs of secure and trustworthy sites, especially if you're entering sensitive information like passwords or credit card details. Here's what to look for:

- **HTTPS vs. HTTP**: Look for "HTTPS" at the beginning of a website's URL instead of "HTTP." The "S" stands for **Secure**, indicating that the site uses encryption to protect data entered on the page. Websites with HTTPS encrypt your information, making it harder for hackers to intercept it.

- **Lock Icon**: In Safari, a small lock icon appears next to the website address if the site is using HTTPS. Tap on the lock icon to view more details about the site's security certificate, which can confirm that you're visiting the legitimate version of a website.
- **Avoiding Suspicious URLs**: Watch for misspelled URLs, extra characters, or random numbers in the web address, as these can indicate fake or malicious sites. Scammers often use slight variations of popular websites to trick users (e.g., "faceb00k.com" instead of "facebook.com").

By checking these indicators, you can quickly assess whether a site is secure and reliable before interacting with it.

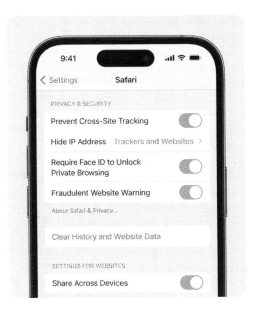

Safari offers a **Private Browsing** mode, which is useful for keeping your browsing history and website data private. When using Private Browsing, Safari won't save your search history, cookies, or form data, providing a layer of privacy that can be helpful when browsing sensitive information. Here's how to use it:

- **Activating Private Browsing**:
  - » Open Safari, then tap the **Tabs** icon (two overlapping squares) in the bottom-right corner. Select **Private** to enable Private Browsing, then tap **Done**.
  - » In Private mode, the Safari interface will turn dark, indicating that your session is private. Any tabs opened in this mode will not be saved once you close them.
- **Benefits of Private Browsing**:
  - » Private Browsing is useful if you're searching for sensitive information, such as health topics or financial details, or if you're using a shared device. It prevents other users from seeing what websites you've visited and keeps temporary data from being stored on your device.

It's worth noting that Private Browsing only hides your browsing activity on your device and does not provide anonymity on the internet. Websites you visit can still see your IP address, and your activity may still be visible to your internet service provider.

Clearing your browsing data regularly helps protect your privacy by removing stored information, such as cookies, cache, and history, from Safari. Here's how to clear your browsing data on the iPhone:

- **Clearing Data in Safari**:
  - » Go to **Settings > Safari**, then scroll down and tap **Clear History and Website Data**. This action deletes your browsing history, cookies, and cache, freeing up storage and reducing tracking by websites.
  - » You can choose to clear specific website data if you don't want to erase everything. Go to **Advanced > Website Data** to view and delete data from individual sites.

Regularly clearing your browsing data prevents websites from tracking your activity over time and helps ensure that your device remains free from unnecessary stored data.

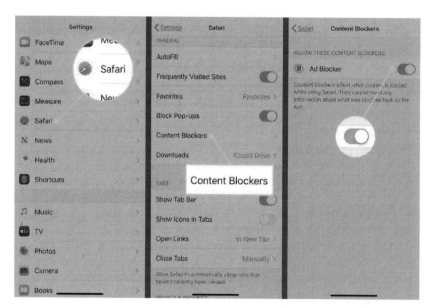

Content blockers are extensions that can block ads, trackers, and other unwanted content on websites. By reducing the amount of data loaded on each page, content blockers can make browsing faster and help protect your privacy. Here's how to set up content blockers:

- **Downloading a Content Blocker**:
  - » To use a content blocker, download one from the App Store, such as AdGuard or Wipr. These apps typically offer customizable settings to control what types of content are blocked.

Enabling Content Blockers in Safari:

 » After downloading a content blocker, go to **Settings > Safari > Content Blockers** and enable the content blocker app. You can enable multiple content blockers if you have more than one installed.

Content blockers enhance security and improve browsing speed by blocking intrusive ads, preventing tracking, and eliminating distractions.

It's essential to be cautious with links and downloads while browsing, as these can sometimes contain malicious software or lead to phishing sites. Here are some tips for avoiding unsafe links and downloads:

- **Avoid Clicking on Suspicious Links**: Be cautious with links sent through email or social media, especially if they come from unknown senders. These links could lead to phishing sites that try to steal your information.
- **Download Only from Trusted Sources**: Avoid downloading software or files from unfamiliar websites, as these may contain viruses or malware. Stick to reputable websites, such as official app stores or verified company websites, when downloading software or files.

By exercising caution with links and downloads, you can protect your device from malware and avoid scams.

Safari's built-in **iCloud Keychain** securely stores your passwords and automatically fills them in when you visit saved websites. This feature makes logging in to websites easier and protects you from phishing sites by ensuring you're on the legitimate website before your password is entered. Here's how to set up and use Keychain:

- **Enabling Keychain**:
  - » Go to **Settings > [Your Name] > iCloud > Keychain** and turn on **iCloud Keychain**. This securely stores your passwords across all Apple devices signed in with your Apple ID.
- **Using Autofill**:
  - » When you visit a site with a saved password, Safari will prompt you to autofill your credentials. Simply tap on the login field and select the suggested login information.
  - » If you need to save a new password, Safari will ask if you'd like to store it in Keychain after you enter it on a website. Storing passwords securely in Keychain reduces the risk of forgetting them and makes logging in faster.

Keychain keeps your passwords secure while helping you avoid unsafe sites, as it won't prompt you to autofill on phishing pages.

Safari's Privacy Report provides insights into how websites track your activity, giving you a better understanding of your online privacy. Here's how to access and interpret it:

- **Viewing the Privacy Report**:
  - » Open Safari, tap the **aA** icon in the address bar, and select **Privacy Report**. This report shows the number of trackers blocked by Safari, the websites with the most trackers, and other details about tracking attempts.
- **Using the Privacy Report to Adjust Browsing Habits**:
  - » Reviewing the Privacy Report can help you identify websites that frequently use trackers, which may indicate that they collect excessive data. You can decide to avoid these websites or use content blockers to minimize tracking.

The Privacy Report empowers you to make informed choices about which sites to trust, helping you protect your privacy and control the data collected about you.

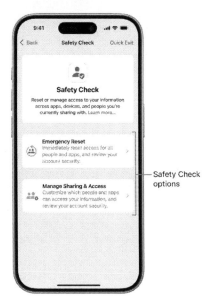

Safety Check options

A few more tips can help you stay safe while browsing with Safari:

- **Log Out of Websites When Finished**: Logging out of websites, especially those with sensitive information like banking sites, adds an extra layer of security by ensuring your account isn't accessible to others if your device is lost or stolen.
- **Avoid Public Wi-Fi for Sensitive Transactions**: Avoid accessing sensitive sites, such as online banking, while connected to public Wi-Fi, which is more vulnerable to security risks. If you must use public Wi-Fi, consider using a Virtual Private Network (VPN) to encrypt your connection.
- **Enable Two-Factor Authentication**: For sites that support it, enable two-factor authentication (2FA) to add an extra layer of security to your accounts. 2FA requires a second form of verification, such as a code sent to your phone, when logging in.

With these tips and Safari's built-in safety features, you can browse the web with confidence. Safari's focus on privacy, security, and ease of use makes it a reliable tool for safe internet browsing. By using these features, practicing safe browsing habits, and being cautious with unfamiliar sites, you can enjoy a secure online experience on your iPhone 16.

Recognizing Scams and Avoiding Spam

In today's digital world, scams and spam are common challenges for internet users. Scams often appear as phishing emails, fake websites, or fraudulent messages designed to trick people into revealing personal information or sending money. Spam, on the other hand, is unsolicited, irrelevant, or unwanted messages that can clutter your inbox and sometimes include harmful links or attachments. This section will guide you through recognizing common scams, avoiding spam, and using your iPhone's tools to protect yourself from online threats.

From: Apple ID >

To: ▆▆▆▆▆▆▆ >   Hide   AL

[Reminder] Your Account was locked and required verification. [Services : 4552667853]

Today at 15:37

Dea▆▆▆▆▆▆▆▆▆▆▆▆

Your Apple ID was locked due to security reasons. We have detected a sign-in from an unknown device and an unusual activity from your account.

Please verify your identity within 24 hours or your account will be disabled due to concerns we have for the safety and integrity of the Apple Community.
Use this link https://appleid.apple.com to verify your account.

Sincerely
Apple

Scammers use various tactics to try to gain access to your personal information or finances. Here are some of the most common types of scams and how to spot them:

- **Phishing Emails and Messages**:
  - » Phishing is one of the most widespread scams. It involves fraudulent emails or messages that appear to be from reputable companies, such as banks, social media sites, or government agencies. These messages often contain urgent language, like "Your account will be suspended," and include links to fake websites that ask for your login credentials.
  - » To recognize phishing, look closely at the sender's email address or phone number. Scammers often use addresses that look similar to legitimate ones but may have slight variations, like extra letters or numbers. Also, be cautious of any messages asking you to "verify" or "confirm" personal information.
- **Fake Invoices or Purchase Confirmations**:
  - » Some scammers send fake invoices or order confirmations that claim you made a purchase. These emails often include links for "cancellations" or "disputes" that lead to phishing sites. For example, you might receive an email claiming to be from Amazon, saying you've bought an expensive item you didn't order.
  - » To avoid falling for these scams, never click on links in suspicious emails. Instead, log in directly to the website (e.g.,

Amazon) and check your recent purchases. Legitimate companies typically include your full name and details of the purchase in confirmation emails, while fake emails are often generic.

- **Tech Support Scams**:
  - » Tech support scams involve calls, emails, or pop-ups claiming that there's an issue with your device, such as a virus or malware infection, and that you need to contact "tech support" to fix it. These scammers often pressure you to pay for fake security services or software.
  - » Remember that legitimate tech support companies, including Apple, will not contact you unsolicited. If you receive a call or message claiming to be from tech support, hang up or ignore it. If you have concerns, contact the company directly using their official website.

- **Prize and Lottery Scams**:
  - » These scams claim you've won a prize or lottery, and all you need to do is provide personal information or pay a small fee to claim it. Scammers often say things like, "Congratulations, you've won $1,000!"
  - » Legitimate contests do not require payment or personal information to claim a prize. If you receive an unsolicited message about a prize, it's best to ignore it.

Spam messages are unsolicited messages that fill up your inbox, often from unknown senders promoting products or services. Here's how to identify spam and take steps to reduce it:

- **Characteristics of Spam Emails**:
  - » Spam emails often have generic greetings like "Dear Customer," misspellings, or unprofessional formatting. They may include promotional content or links to unknown websites. These messages are often sent from unknown email addresses.
  - » Spam messages may also use language that pressures you to act quickly, such as "Limited time offer" or "Act now." These tactics are designed to capture your attention and encourage you to click on links or respond.

- **Unsubscribing from Legitimate Marketing Emails**:
  - » If you're receiving too many emails from a particular company, most legitimate businesses include an **Unsubscribe** link at the bottom of their emails. By clicking on this link, you can remove yourself from their mailing list.
  - » Be cautious with the unsubscribe option if the email appears suspicious. Scammers sometimes use fake "unsubscribe" links to confirm that your email address is active. For legitimate emails, look for unsubscribe options that lead to recognizable, trusted sites.

- **Avoiding Unnecessary Sign-Ups**:
  - » Many websites ask for your email address to access content or services, which can lead to an influx of promotional

emails. To reduce spam, avoid signing up on sites you don't fully trust or consider using a secondary email address for non-essential subscriptions.

Your iPhone offers several built-in tools and settings to help manage spam and protect you from scams. Here's how to make use of these features:

- **Mail's Junk Filter**:
  - » The Mail app has a built-in junk filter that automatically detects and moves spam emails to the Junk folder. To check for spam, open the Mail app and navigate to **Junk**. If you find a legitimate email in Junk, you can mark it as "Not Junk" to ensure future emails from that sender go to your inbox.
  - » Over time, marking emails as junk or not junk improves the filter's accuracy, helping you keep spam out of your inbox.

- **Blocking Unwanted Senders**:
  - » If you repeatedly receive unwanted messages from a specific sender, you can block them. Open the email, tap on the sender's name, and select **Block This Contact**. Blocked senders' messages will go directly to your Junk folder, reducing clutter in your inbox.

- **Reporting Phishing Emails**:
  - » If you receive a phishing email, report it to Apple by forwarding it to **reportphishing@apple.com**. Many email providers also have phishing-reporting tools, which can help them filter out similar messages in the future.

Being cautious when browsing can help protect you from scams and malware:

- **Checking Links Before Clicking**:
  - » Hover over links (by pressing and holding on a link in the email or message) to see the URL destination before clicking. This technique helps you identify suspicious links. If a link doesn't match the sender's legitimate website (e.g., an email from "PayPal" links to a random site), it's best to avoid it.

- **Using Safari's Fraudulent Website Warning**:
  - » Safari includes a Fraudulent Website Warning feature, which alerts you when you try to visit a site known for phishing or scams. Ensure this feature is enabled in **Settings > Safari** by toggling on **Fraudulent Website Warning**.

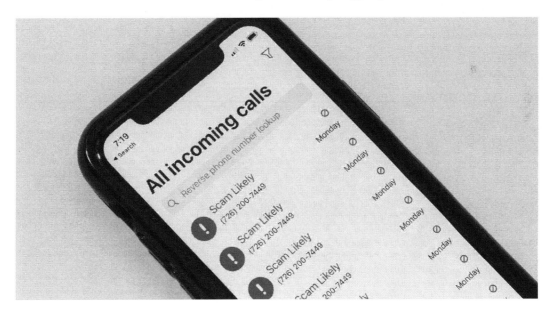

Developing safe online habits can protect you from most scams and spam. Here are some best practices:

- **Do Not Share Personal Information**:
  - » Legitimate companies won't ask for personal information like passwords or social security numbers through email or text. If you receive such a request, don't respond. Instead, contact the company directly through its official website or app.

- **Avoid Clicking on Attachments or Links from Unknown Senders**:

- » Attachments from unknown senders can contain malware that compromises your device's security. Avoid downloading attachments or clicking links from untrusted sources.
- **Use Strong Passwords and Two-Factor Authentication**:
  - » Protect your accounts with unique, strong passwords for each service, and enable two-factor authentication (2FA) whenever available. 2FA provides an extra layer of security by requiring an additional code to log in, reducing the chance of unauthorized access.
- **Beware of Pressure Tactics**:
  - » Scammers often create a sense of urgency, saying things like, "Act now!" or "Your account will be suspended." Take your time before responding, and don't let pressure tactics push you into clicking on a link or providing information.

If you continue to receive a lot of spam, third-party apps can add another layer of protection. Some reputable spam-blocking apps available for iPhone include:

- **Hiya**: Hiya blocks spam calls and identifies potentially fraudulent numbers. It also offers reverse phone number lookup features.
- **Truecaller**: Truecaller is popular for its spam-blocking features and community-based database of known scam numbers. It can identify unknown callers and automatically block spam.

After downloading a spam-blocking app, go to **Settings > Phone > Call Blocking & Identification** to enable it. Many of these apps require a subscription for full features but can significantly reduce spam if you get frequent spam calls or messages.

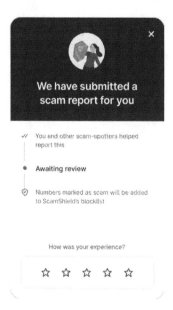

If you encounter a particularly aggressive or sophisticated scam, report it to the appropriate authorities. In the U.S., you can report scams to the **Federal Trade Commission (FTC)** at **www.ftc.gov/complaint**. Reporting scams helps government agencies track and prevent fraud and raises awareness of new scams that target individuals.

By being vigilant and using the tools and techniques provided by your iPhone, you can protect yourself from scams and spam. From recognizing common tactics used by scammers to managing unwanted messages with spam filters, these steps create a safer digital environment. By following these practices, you can enjoy a more secure and spam-free online experience on your iPhone.

Managing Privacy and App Permissions

In our digital age, protecting personal privacy has become more important than ever. Apps and websites often request access to sensitive information, like your location, contacts, photos, and microphone. While granting permissions to trusted apps can enhance their functionality, it's essential to understand and control what data you share to ensure your privacy and security. Your iPhone 16 includes built-in tools and settings to manage app permissions, control data sharing, and protect your privacy. This section will guide you through how to manage privacy settings effectively, review and adjust app permissions, and take additional steps to keep your data secure.

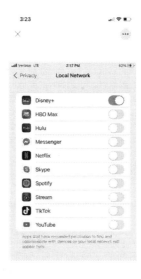

App permissions allow apps to access specific features or information on your iPhone, such as the camera, location, contacts, and photos. Here's why managing these permissions is essential:

- **Privacy Protection**: Some apps collect data unnecessarily or may use it in ways that aren't immediately clear. By carefully controlling permissions, you can limit what apps can access, ensuring your personal information stays private.
- **Enhanced Security**: Apps with unnecessary permissions can expose you to security risks. For instance, if a third-party app has access to your contacts or photos and gets hacked, your data could be exposed. Limiting permissions minimizes the potential for data misuse.
- **Better Device Performance**: Some permissions, like those that track your location, can drain battery life and use extra data. By allowing permissions only when necessary, you can optimize device performance and conserve battery.

Taking control of app permissions means you're in charge of what information is shared, which helps maintain privacy and minimize security risks.

Your iPhone allows you to review and adjust app permissions in the Settings app. Here's how to manage permissions for each app individually:

- **Reviewing Permissions for Individual Apps**:
  - » Go to **Settings** and scroll down to find the app whose permissions you want to review. Tap on the app to see which permissions it currently has access to, such as **Location**, **Photos**, **Camera**, **Microphone**, and **Contacts**.
  - » To adjust any permission, tap on it. For instance, if an app has access to your location, you'll see options like **Never**, **Ask Next Time or When I Share**, **While Using the App**, and **Always**. Choose the option that best suits your privacy needs.

- **Managing Permissions by Category**:
  - » If you want to see which apps have access to a specific type of information, go to **Settings > Privacy & Security**. Here, you'll find categories like **Location Services**, **Contacts**, **Photos**, and **Microphone**.
  - » Tap on any category to see the list of apps that have requested permission for that specific feature. For example, selecting **Camera** will show all apps that have requested access to your camera. You can turn permissions on or off for each app individually.

Some permissions are more sensitive than others and should be managed with extra caution:

Location Services:

» Location access is one of the most requested permissions, but not all apps genuinely need it. To manage this setting, go to **Settings > Privacy & Security > Location Services**.

» You can choose from different options for each app:

Never: The app will not access your location at all.

Ask Next Time or When I Share: The app will prompt you each time it wants to access your location, giving you control on a per-use basis.

While Using the App: The app can access your location only when it's open and in use.

Always: The app has access to your location at all times, even in the background.

» Limiting location access to "While Using the App" is often a good choice, as it prevents background tracking and helps conserve battery.

Photos and Camera:

» Photo and camera access can be very personal, so it's essential to control which apps have access to your images. Go to **Settings > Privacy & Security > Photos** to view apps with access to your photos.

» You can choose **Selected Photos** to allow the app access to only specific photos, or **None** if the app doesn't need access to your photos. For the Camera, go to **Settings > Privacy & Security > Camera** to review and adjust camera access.

Microphone:

» Many apps request microphone access, especially social media and video apps. However, you should limit microphone permissions to apps where it's absolutely necessary, such as voice calling or video recording apps.

» Go to **Settings > Privacy & Security > Microphone** to see which apps have microphone access and toggle them off for apps you don't trust or use infrequently.

Contacts and Calendar:

» Access to contacts and calendar events can help some apps (like messaging or scheduling apps) function better, but it's a good idea to limit these permissions to trusted apps only. Go to **Settings > Privacy & Security > Contacts** and **Calendar** to review access and turn off permissions for unnecessary apps.

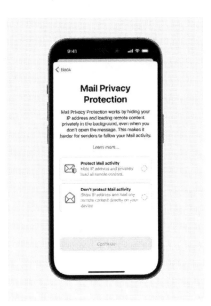

Apple has implemented additional privacy tools that give you greater control over your data and provide transparency about how apps use your information:

App Privacy Labels:

» In the App Store, every app includes a **Privacy Label** that discloses what types of data it collects. This label is similar to a "nutrition label" for privacy and lets you see if the app collects data like location, contacts, browsing history, or financial information.

» Review these labels before downloading an app, especially if it requests access to sensitive data. Apps that collect minimal data or don't track users are often a safer choice.

- **App Tracking Transparency (ATT)**:

» App Tracking Transparency (ATT) allows you to choose whether apps can track your activity across other companies' apps and websites. When you open an app for the first time, a prompt will appear asking for permission to "Allow Tracking."

» You can either allow tracking or select "Ask App Not to Track." Most apps can function without tracking, so denying this request enhances your privacy. To manage ATT settings for all apps, go to **Settings > Privacy & Security > Tracking** and toggle off **Allow Apps to Request to Track**.

If you're concerned about privacy while browsing the internet, Safari includes several privacy features that can help:

- **Intelligent Tracking Prevention**:

» Safari's **Intelligent Tracking Prevention** automatically blocks third-party tracking cookies, which are used to follow your browsing activity across websites. This feature helps prevent advertisers from building a profile based on your browsing habits.

- **Privacy Report**:

» Safari provides a **Privacy Report** showing how many trackers have been blocked in the past 30 days. To access this report, open Safari, tap the **aA** icon in the address bar, and select **Privacy Report**. This feature gives you insight into which websites are using trackers, empowering you to make informed decisions about where you browse.

- **Private Browsing**:

» When using **Private Browsing** mode, Safari won't save your browsing history, cookies, or website data. This mode is useful for searching sensitive information and ensures that your browsing activity isn't stored on your device.

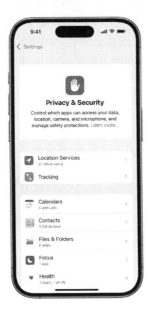

Some apps continually track location in the background, which can compromise privacy and drain battery life. Use these steps to limit unnecessary location tracking:

- **Limit System Services Location Access**:

  » Go to **Settings > Privacy & Security > Location Services > System Services** to review system services that use location tracking. Features like **Location-Based Ads** and **Location-Based Suggestions** are not essential, so turning them off can improve privacy.

- **View Recent Location Access**:

  » You can see which apps have accessed your location recently by looking at the **Location Services** page. Apps with a purple arrow have recently accessed your location, while apps with a gray arrow have used your location within the past 24 hours. If an app frequently accesses your location without reason, consider adjusting its permissions.

Using iCloud Keychain can help protect sensitive information, such as passwords and credit card details, by securely storing and auto-filling them on trusted websites and apps:

- **Enabling iCloud Keychain**:

  » Go to **Settings > [Your Name] > iCloud > Keychain** and toggle it on. This feature securely stores your passwords across Apple devices linked to your Apple ID, making it convenient to log in without compromising security.

- **Reviewing Password Security Recommendations**:
  - » In **Settings > Passwords**, you can view a list of saved passwords and see if any are considered weak or reused. Tap on **Security Recommendations** to update vulnerable passwords and improve account security.

A few more privacy practices can further enhance your security:

- **Use Two-Factor Authentication (2FA)**: For additional security, enable **2FA** for your Apple ID and other accounts. 2FA requires a verification code along with your password, providing an extra layer of protection against unauthorized access.
- **Regularly Review App Permissions**: Check app permissions periodically to ensure only essential apps have access to your data. Over time, some apps may no longer need certain permissions, so adjusting them helps maintain optimal privacy.
- **Limit Exposure on Social Media**: Many social media apps request extensive permissions. Review these permissions and limit unnecessary ones, such as access to location, microphone, and contacts, to reduce the potential for data sharing.

By following these practices and taking advantage of your iPhone's privacy tools, you'll be better equipped to protect your personal information and control how your data is shared. Managing app permissions, adjusting privacy settings, and staying aware of data-sharing practices are essential steps in maintaining a secure, private digital experience on your iPhone 16.

CHAPTER 7
ADVANCED COMMUNICATION TOOLS

Welcome to Chapter 7: Advanced Communication Tools! Your iPhone 16 offers powerful tools to enhance your connections, from staying in touch with loved ones through video calls to setting up emergency features that provide peace of mind. In this chapter, we'll explore these advanced tools, showing you how to get the most out of FaceTime, group messaging, and emergency features, so you can communicate and stay safe with confidence.

We'll begin with **FaceTime**, Apple's built-in video calling app that allows you to make face-to-face calls with friends, family, and colleagues, no matter where they are. FaceTime's high-quality video and audio make it ideal for everything from quick check-ins to lengthy conversations. You'll learn how to make and receive FaceTime calls, add multiple people to a call for group video chats, and even enhance your calls with fun effects like filters and stickers.

Next, we'll cover **group messaging and multimedia sharing**. Group messaging lets you communicate with multiple people in one chat, making it easy to coordinate plans, share photos, and keep up with family conversations. We'll walk through how to start group chats, customize settings, share multimedia content, and use tools like reactions and replies to keep conversations organized and engaging. Whether you're sharing photos, videos, or just chatting with a group, these features make staying connected more enjoyable and convenient.

Finally, we'll discuss **Emergency SOS and Medical ID**—two features designed to keep you safe in case of emergencies. With Emergency SOS, you can quickly call for help by pressing a few buttons, and the Medical ID feature provides first responders with important health information if needed. We'll show you how to set up both features, ensuring that you're prepared and secure in unexpected situations.

By mastering these advanced communication tools, you'll unlock new ways to connect, share, and stay safe. FaceTime and group messaging will make daily communication more interactive, while the Emergency SOS and Medical ID features provide essential support in critical moments. Let's dive into this chapter and make sure your iPhone is set up to keep you connected and protected, whether you're chatting with loved ones or navigating an emergency.

FaceTime for Video Calling

FaceTime is Apple's built-in video calling app, designed to make staying in touch easy and personal by allowing face-to-face conversations from anywhere. Whether you're connecting with family across the country, chatting with friends, or joining a remote meeting, FaceTime provides high-quality video and audio, making it feel like everyone is in the same room. This section will walk you through using FaceTime for one-on-one calls, setting up group FaceTime calls, and using fun features like effects, screen sharing, and even using FaceTime with Android or Windows users.

FaceTime is pre-installed on your iPhone, and getting started with it is simple:

- **Opening FaceTime**: To open FaceTime, locate the **FaceTime** app on your Home Screen or in the App Library. Tap the app to open the main screen, where you can start new calls, view recent calls, and access additional settings.
- **Setting Up FaceTime**: If you're using FaceTime for the first time, go to **Settings > FaceTime** to ensure it's enabled. Here, you can choose to be reachable by FaceTime through your phone number or Apple ID email. This setting lets others contact you on FaceTime using either method.

Making a FaceTime call is straightforward and can be done in a few taps:

- **Starting a Call from the FaceTime App**:
  - » Open the **FaceTime** app, then tap the **New FaceTime** button (a plus sign in a circle).
  - » Enter the name, phone number, or email address of the person you want to call. If they're an Apple user with Face-Time, you'll see an option to make a **Video** or **Audio** call.
  - » Tap **FaceTime Video** to start a video call, or choose **FaceTime Audio** if you only need audio. FaceTime Audio is a great alternative to a regular phone call, offering high-quality sound over Wi-Fi.
- **Starting a Call from the Contacts or Messages App**:
  - » You can also start a FaceTime call directly from your Contacts or Messages app. Open a conversation or contact, tap the **FaceTime** icon, and select **Video** or **Audio** to start a call.

Answering a FaceTime Call:

» When someone FaceTimes you, a notification appears on your screen, similar to an incoming phone call. To answer, tap **Accept**. If you can't take the call, you can tap **Decline** to dismiss it.

Group FaceTime lets you add multiple people to a call, making it perfect for family catch-ups, virtual hangouts, or team meetings. Here's how to set up and use Group FaceTime:

- **Starting a Group FaceTime Call**:

  » Open the FaceTime app and tap **New FaceTime**. Add the contacts of everyone you want to include, then tap **Face-Time** to start the call. Group FaceTime supports up to 32 participants, allowing you to include a large number of friends or family members.

- **Adding People to an Existing FaceTime Call**:

  » If you're already on a FaceTime call and want to add more people, tap the screen to bring up the options menu, then swipe up and select **Add People**. Enter the contact details of the person you'd like to add and tap **Add to FaceTime**. This feature is useful if you want to include someone else in the conversation mid-call.

- **Managing Group FaceTime Views**:

  » In Group FaceTime, each person's video feed appears as a tile on the screen. By default, FaceTime automatically resizes tiles based on who's speaking. You can tap on a person's tile to make their video larger, ensuring you focus on specific participants when needed.

FaceTime includes effects, filters, and Memoji (animated emojis that look like you) to make calls more fun and engaging. These features can add a playful touch, especially during calls with friends and family:

- **Adding Filters**:
  - » During a FaceTime call, tap on the screen, then tap the **Effects** icon (a star). Choose **Filters** to access options that change the color or style of your video feed, such as "Comic Book" or "Black and White." Filters are a fun way to add a unique look to your video, and they can lighten the mood on social calls.

- **Using Memoji and Animoji**:
  - » Memoji and Animoji let you appear as an animated character, such as a cartoon version of yourself or an animal. To use them, tap the **Effects** icon, select **Memoji**, and choose the character you want. Your Memoji will move and react based on your facial expressions, adding a touch of humor and creativity to your calls.

- **Adding Text and Stickers**:
  - » FaceTime allows you to add text or stickers on the screen. Tap **Effects**, select **Text**, and type your message, which will appear over your video. This feature is great for adding captions or fun phrases to your video feed.

With the release of iOS 15, Apple made FaceTime available to Android and Windows users via web links. Here's how to invite non-Apple users to join a FaceTime call:

- **Creating a FaceTime Link**:
  - » Open the FaceTime app and tap **Create Link**. You can then share the link through Messages, Mail, or other apps, allowing Android and Windows users to join your call by clicking the link.
- **Joining the Call**:
  - » When the recipient opens the link, they'll be able to join the FaceTime call through a browser. You'll need to accept their request to join the call, which gives you control over who enters your video session.

This feature makes FaceTime more versatile, allowing you to connect with people on other platforms while still enjoying FaceTime's secure and high-quality calling experience.

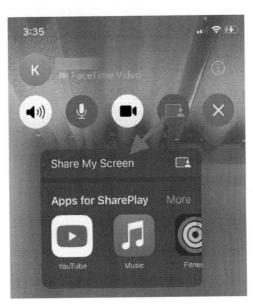

Screen sharing is a helpful feature for showing someone else what's on your screen. Whether you're helping a family member navigate their settings, sharing a photo album, or presenting a document, screen sharing makes it easy to guide others visually:

- **Starting Screen Sharing**:
  - » During a FaceTime call, tap on the screen to bring up options, then tap the **Share Screen** icon (a rectangle with a person). Your screen will be shared with everyone on the call, allowing them to see exactly what you're viewing.
  - » While screen sharing, you can navigate through apps, photos, or documents, and the other participants will follow along in real-time. Tap **Stop Sharing** to end screen sharing and return to the regular video call.

Screen sharing is especially useful for troubleshooting, showing family members how to use their devices, or collaborating on work projects.

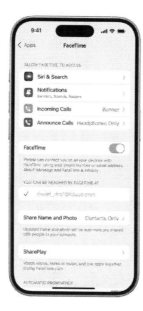

FaceTime's quality depends on your internet connection, so here are some tips to enhance your calling experience:

- **Use Wi-Fi Over Cellular Data**: For the best video quality, connect to a strong Wi-Fi network. FaceTime works over cellular data, but video quality may be lower, especially if the connection is slow.
- **Close Background Apps**: To free up resources, close other apps running in the background, as they may impact FaceTime's performance. Swiping up from the bottom of the screen and closing unnecessary apps can help ensure FaceTime runs smoothly.
- **Check Lighting and Positioning**: Good lighting makes a big difference in video quality. Try to have a light source in front of you, like a window or lamp, to ensure you're well-lit. Hold your phone at eye level and make sure your face is visible in the frame.

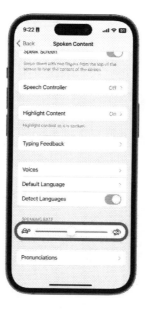

Apple includes several accessibility features in FaceTime to make it more user-friendly for everyone:

- **Sign Language Detection**: In Group FaceTime, FaceTime can detect when someone is using sign language and automatically make their tile larger, making it easier for others to focus on them.
- **Closed Captions**: For individuals who may have hearing impairments, enabling **Closed Captions** provides real-time subtitles for calls, helping everyone stay engaged.

FaceTime is built with security in mind, and all FaceTime calls are end-to-end encrypted. This means that only you and the people on your call can see and hear what's being shared. Apple cannot access FaceTime calls, so you can rest assured that your conversations are private and secure.

If you receive unwanted FaceTime calls, you can block the caller. Go to **Settings > FaceTime > Blocked Contacts**, where you can add numbers or contacts to your blocked list. This feature helps prevent spam or unsolicited calls, ensuring a safe and secure experience.

FaceTime is a versatile tool that allows you to connect with friends, family, and colleagues in meaningful ways, no matter the distance. From individual calls to large group chats, FaceTime's features make communication personal, fun, and effective. By learning to make and manage calls, add effects, share screens, and connect with non-Apple users, you can unlock the full potential of FaceTime, bringing those you care about closer through high-quality video calls. Whether you're having a quick chat or hosting a virtual family reunion, FaceTime is a powerful tool for staying connected and enhancing your relationships.

Group Messaging and Multimedia Sharing

Group messaging and multimedia sharing are powerful tools for staying connected with multiple people at once, whether you're planning a family gathering, coordinating with friends, or collaborating with colleagues. The iPhone 16's Messages app makes group communication engaging and easy to manage, providing a range of features that allow you to create group chats, share multimedia content, and organize conversations. This section will guide you through the basics of setting up group messages, sharing photos, videos, and other media, and using advanced tools like reactions, mentions, and notifications to keep everyone in the loop.

Setting up a group message in the Messages app allows you to communicate with multiple people in a single chat, making it easy to organize events, share updates, or simply stay in touch. Here's how to get started:

- **Starting a New Group Message**:
  - » Open the **Messages** app and tap the **Compose** icon (a square with a pencil). In the **To** field, enter the names or phone numbers of the people you want to include in the group chat.
  - » Once you've added everyone, type your message in the text box and tap **Send** to start the conversation. You can include as many participants as needed, and each person in the chat will receive your message at the same time.

- **Naming the Group**:
  - » To make it easier to recognize your group chats, you can give each one a unique name. Open the group conversation, tap the **Contact Icons** at the top of the screen, then select **Change Name and Photo**.
  - » Enter a name for the group and, if desired, set a custom group photo or emoji. Naming the group is especially helpful for keeping track of different chats if you're part of multiple group conversations.

- **Customizing Group Settings**:
  - » In a group chat, you can customize settings to suit your needs. Tap the group's name or icon at the top of the conversation to access options like **Hide Alerts** (which silences notifications for the group), **Leave This Conversation** (if you want to exit the group), or **Add Contact** (to include additional people).
  - » These options give you control over your group conversations, allowing you to stay involved without unnecessary interruptions or add new members as needed.

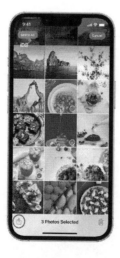 

One of the key features of group messaging is the ability to share multimedia content, making conversations more engaging and dynamic. Here's how to share photos, videos, and other media in a group chat:

- **Sending Photos and Videos**:
  - » To share a photo or video, tap the **Camera** icon next to the text box. You can either take a new photo or video directly in the Messages app or choose one from your gallery by tapping the **Photos** icon.
  - » After selecting a photo or video, you can add an optional caption and tap **Send**. This content will appear in the group chat for all participants to view and download. Shared photos and videos are great for keeping everyone updated, whether you're sharing family photos, vacation snapshots, or highlights from an event.
- **Sharing Links and Documents**:
  - » In addition to photos and videos, you can also share links to websites, news articles, or documents. To share a link, simply copy it from your browser, paste it into the message field, and tap **Send**.
  - » For documents or files, tap the **Files** icon in the Messages app to browse files on your device or in iCloud Drive. Sharing documents is particularly useful for work-related group chats or organizing event details.
- **Using Tapbacks and Reactions**:
  - » In group messages, quick reactions (called **Tapbacks**) allow you to respond to specific messages with a simple icon, such as a thumbs-up, heart, or laugh. To add a Tapback, press and hold on the message you want to react to, then select an icon from the list.
  - » Tapbacks are a quick way to acknowledge messages without sending a new text, keeping the conversation streamlined while letting others know you've seen or appreciated their message.

Mentions and inline replies help you keep group chats organized and focused, especially in busy conversations with multiple people. Here's how to use these features:

- **Mentions**:
  - » Mentions let you direct a message to a specific person in the group. To mention someone, type @ followed by their name (e.g., "@John"). The person you mention will receive a notification, making it easier for them to catch up on messages that directly involve them.
  - » Mentions are helpful for getting someone's attention or addressing specific points without having to wait for them to scroll through the entire conversation.
- **Inline Replies**:
  - » Inline replies allow you to respond directly to a specific message, creating a mini-thread within the conversation. To use an inline reply, press and hold the message you want to reply to, then select **Reply**. Type your response, and it will appear as a nested reply under the original message.

» Inline replies make group chats easier to follow by keeping responses to specific messages organized, which is especially useful when multiple topics are being discussed at once.

With group messages, notifications can quickly become overwhelming. Fortunately, the Messages app allows you to customize alerts for group chats:

- **Hiding Alerts**:

  » If you want to mute notifications for a group chat without leaving the conversation, you can use the **Hide Alerts** feature. Open the group chat, tap the **Contact Icons** at the top, and toggle **Hide Alerts**. You'll still receive messages, but without constant notifications.

  » Hiding alerts is perfect for staying in the loop without being distracted by every new message, especially in larger group chats.

- **Notifications for Mentions Only**:

  » For groups where you want to stay informed but don't need to see every message, you can set notifications to only appear when you're mentioned. Go to **Settings > Messages** and toggle on **Notify Me** for mentions. With this setting, you'll only receive notifications when someone tags you directly, making it easier to prioritize relevant messages.

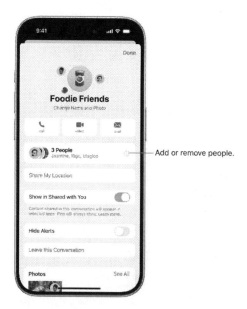

Add or remove people.

As group conversations grow, it can be challenging to find specific information or messages. The Messages app includes helpful tools for organizing and locating messages:

- **Using Search in Messages**:
  - » To find a particular message, open the Messages app and tap the **Search Bar** at the top. Enter keywords related to what you're looking for, and Messages will display relevant results from all your chats, including group messages.
  - » The search function is especially useful for locating past conversations, shared links, or important details without scrolling through long chats.
- **Viewing Shared Media in Group Chats**:
  - » Each group chat has a section where you can view all the photos, videos, and links shared within the conversation. Open the group chat, tap the **Contact Icons** at the top, and scroll down to **Photos** and **Links**.
  - » This feature allows you to browse all shared content in one place, making it easier to find that important document, photo, or video without scrolling through individual messages.

For times when texting isn't enough, you can switch from a group chat to a FaceTime call with just a few taps:

- **Starting a Group FaceTime Call**:
  - » Open the group chat, tap the **Contact Icons** at the top, and select **FaceTime** to initiate a video or audio call with everyone in the conversation. Group FaceTime supports up to 32 participants, so it's perfect for larger family or friend gatherings.
  - » FaceTime allows you to transition smoothly from text to live conversation, making group communication more dynamic and engaging.

7. Tips for Enhancing Group Communication

Using group messaging and multimedia sharing effectively can make communication more enjoyable and efficient. Here are some additional tips:

- **Set Ground Rules for Large Groups**: For large groups, consider setting basic guidelines, like limiting messages to specific times or topics, to keep the conversation organized and respectful of everyone's time.
- **Share Important Updates via Inline Replies**: When you're sharing important updates or announcements, using inline replies can help keep these messages organized, especially if multiple topics are discussed within the same group.
- **Use Reactions to Avoid Message Overload**: Tapbacks are a quick way to respond without cluttering the chat, so encourage group members to use them when appropriate. This reduces the number of individual "thanks" or "got it" replies.

The iPhone 16's Messages app makes group communication engaging, efficient, and enjoyable. By using group messages, multimedia sharing, and advanced tools like mentions and inline replies, you can stay connected with friends, family, and colleagues in dynamic ways. Whether you're organizing an event, keeping up with family, or collaborating on a project, these features ensure that everyone is in the loop, conversations are organized, and communication is smooth and interactive. Embracing these tools will enhance your group messaging experience, making it easier and more enjoyable to stay connected.

Emergency SOS and Setting Up Medical ID

Your iPhone 16 includes vital features designed to help in emergencies: Emergency SOS and Medical ID. These tools provide quick access to emergency services and share critical medical information with first responders, offering peace of mind and potentially life-saving support when it matters most. In this section, we'll guide you through setting up and using Emergency SOS and Medical ID, ensuring your iPhone is ready to assist you in urgent situations.

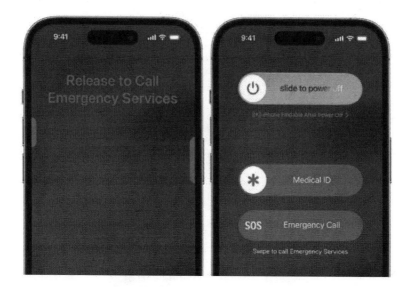

Emergency SOS is a feature that allows you to call emergency services quickly by pressing a combination of buttons on your iPhone. In situations where you may not have time to unlock your phone or dial a number, Emergency SOS provides immediate access to help with just a few button presses. Activating Emergency SOS also notifies your designated emergency contacts, keeping loved ones informed during critical moments.

The Emergency SOS feature is especially useful in scenarios where time is of the essence, such as medical emergencies, accidents, or situations that pose a threat to personal safety. By ensuring that Emergency SOS is set up on your iPhone, you can call for help swiftly, even if you're unable to access the phone normally.

Setting up Emergency SOS on your iPhone 16 is simple and involves enabling specific settings to ensure that the feature is ready whenever you need it:

- **Enabling Emergency SOS:**

- » Go to **Settings > Emergency SOS**. Here, you'll find options like **Call with Hold** and **Call with 5 Presses**.
- » **Call with Hold** allows you to activate Emergency SOS by pressing and holding the side button and either volume button for a few seconds. A countdown will appear on the screen, and if you keep holding the buttons until the countdown ends, your iPhone will automatically call emergency services.
- » **Call with 5 Presses** allows you to initiate Emergency SOS by pressing the side button five times quickly. This feature is beneficial if holding buttons is difficult in an emergency, giving you another way to activate the call.

- **Using Emergency SOS in an Emergency**:
  - » To use Emergency SOS, either press and hold the side button and a volume button, or press the side button five times, depending on which options you've enabled.
  - » Your iPhone will start a loud countdown, giving you a chance to cancel the call if it was triggered accidentally. If you don't cancel, the phone will automatically dial emergency services and alert your emergency contacts.

- **Automatic Notifications to Emergency Contacts**:
  - » When Emergency SOS is activated, your iPhone will notify your designated emergency contacts with your location, keeping them informed of your whereabouts. This notification is crucial for ensuring that loved ones are aware of your situation and can provide assistance if needed.

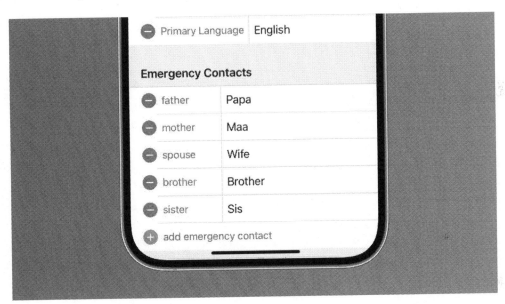

Your emergency contacts are the people who will be alerted if you activate Emergency SOS. These contacts are selected in the Health app and linked to your Medical ID, ensuring they receive an alert when Emergency SOS is used.

- **Adding Emergency Contacts**:
  - » Open the **Health** app, tap on **Medical ID** in the bottom right corner, and select **Edit**.
  - » Scroll down to **Emergency Contacts** and tap **Add Emergency Contact**. Choose the contact you'd like to designate, then select their relationship to you. You can add multiple contacts if desired.
  - » Emergency contacts will receive a notification if Emergency SOS is activated, along with updates on your location until you disable SOS mode.

- **Editing or Removing Emergency Contacts**:
  - » You can edit or remove emergency contacts in the same way by tapping **Edit** in the Medical ID section of the Health app. Keeping this information updated ensures that the right people are contacted in emergencies.

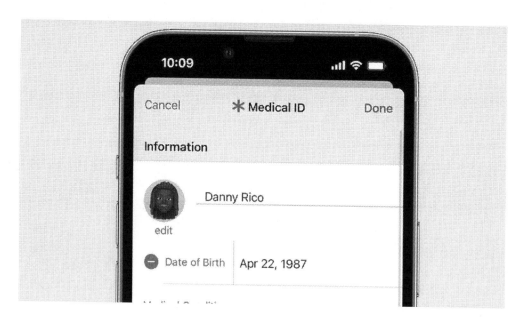

The Medical ID feature on your iPhone provides essential health information to first responders, even from the Lock Screen. Medical ID can include details such as allergies, medical conditions, medications, blood type, and emergency contacts. This information can help medical professionals provide better care if you're unable to communicate in an emergency.

- **Creating Your Medical ID**:
  - » Open the **Health** app, tap **Medical ID**, and then tap **Create Medical ID** if it's your first time setting it up.
  - » Enter relevant information, including your name, date of birth, medical conditions, allergies, medications, blood type, and any other details that may assist first responders.

- **Enabling Access from the Lock Screen**:
  - » At the top of the Medical ID screen, toggle on **Show When Locked**. This setting allows your Medical ID to be accessible from the Lock Screen, ensuring that medical professionals can see critical information without needing to unlock your phone.
  - » This feature can be life-saving in situations where you're unconscious or unable to communicate. First responders can access your Medical ID by swiping up on the Lock Screen, selecting **Emergency**, and tapping **Medical ID**.

- **Keeping Medical ID Updated**:
  - » Regularly review and update your Medical ID, especially if your medical information changes. Up-to-date information ensures that first responders receive accurate details about your health and medications.

In an emergency, knowing how to use Emergency SOS and Medical ID can make a difference. Here's a quick guide to how they work in real-life scenarios:

- **Activating Emergency SOS**:
  - » In any urgent situation, whether it's a health crisis, an accident, or a personal safety issue, you can activate Emergency SOS quickly. If you're unsure about the severity of the situation, it's still okay to activate SOS; emergency services would rather respond to a false alarm than miss a real one.
- **First Responders Accessing Your Medical ID**:
  - » When first responders arrive, they can view your Medical ID by accessing your phone's Lock Screen. They'll see any critical medical information you've entered, helping them understand your needs quickly and act accordingly.
- **Cancelling an Accidental SOS Call**:
  - » If you accidentally activate Emergency SOS, you can cancel the call during the countdown. After the call connects, you can inform emergency services that it was accidental, and they will end the call. It's better to inform them, so they don't dispatch help unnecessarily.

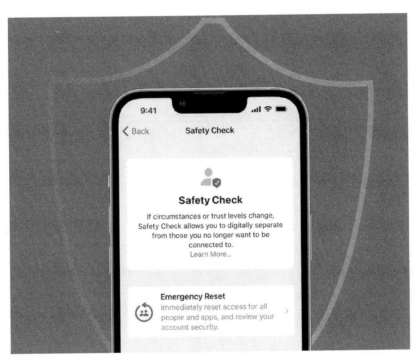

Emergency SOS and Medical ID are designed with privacy and security in mind. Here's how your information is protected:

- **Medical ID Visibility**:
  - » When enabled to show on the Lock Screen, only the information you choose to share will be visible. You have control over what medical information appears, and it's accessible only when someone views your Medical ID from the Lock Screen.
- **Location Sharing with Emergency Contacts**:
  - » When you activate Emergency SOS, your iPhone temporarily shares your location with emergency contacts. This sharing remains active only while SOS mode is enabled, and it stops when you exit SOS mode.

Staying prepared involves more than just setting up Emergency SOS and Medical ID. Here are a few extra steps you can take:

- **Familiarize Yourself with SOS Activation**:
  - » Practice activating Emergency SOS by gently pressing the buttons without fully completing the call. Familiarity with the button sequence helps you act quickly in real situations.

- **Update Emergency Contacts**:
  - » Periodically review and update your emergency contacts. Make sure each contact is aware that they are listed as an emergency contact on your iPhone, so they're prepared to respond if they receive an SOS alert.

- **Discuss Medical ID with Family**:
  - » Let family members or friends know that you've set up Medical ID on your iPhone and explain how it can be accessed. In emergencies, this can ensure they know where to find your critical health information.

Some questions often come up when setting up these emergency features:

- **Will Emergency SOS Work Without Wi-Fi or Cellular?**
  - » Yes, Emergency SOS works over any available cellular network. If no cellular connection is available, it will attempt to connect to any compatible network within range.

- **Is Emergency SOS Available Everywhere?**

» Emergency SOS is available in most regions, but certain features may vary based on local regulations and emergency systems.

- **Can Medical ID Replace a Medical Alert Bracelet?**

   » While Medical ID provides quick access to medical information, some individuals may still prefer medical alert bracelets for visible identification. Medical ID is a helpful supplement but may not fully replace traditional medical alerts for everyone.

Emergency SOS and Medical ID on your iPhone 16 are powerful tools for protecting your safety and well-being. By setting up these features, you're preparing yourself to quickly call for help and provide critical information in emergencies. Whether it's notifying loved ones, alerting emergency services, or sharing health details with first responders, these tools empower you to stay safe and supported in urgent situations. With just a few minutes of setup, you'll have peace of mind knowing your iPhone is ready to assist when you need it most.

CHAPTER 8
DOWNLOADING AND MANAGING APPS

Welcome to Chapter 8: Downloading and Managing Apps! Your iPhone 16 is more than a communication device—it's a versatile tool that can enhance your daily life in numerous ways through the use of apps. From staying on top of your health to exploring hobbies and staying entertained, there are countless apps available that cater to your interests and needs. This chapter will guide you through finding, downloading, organizing, and managing apps to make the most of your iPhone's potential.

We'll begin by exploring the **App Store**, Apple's digital marketplace for applications. The App Store is where you'll find apps for nearly every purpose, from practical tools like weather and health tracking to entertainment apps for movies, music, and games. You'll learn how to navigate the App Store, search for apps, and read reviews, so you can confidently download the ones that meet your needs and interests. Understanding how to assess an app's features and reputation helps you choose the best options and avoid low-quality or irrelevant apps.

Next, we'll discuss **organizing, deleting, and updating apps**. As you start using more apps, keeping your Home Screen tidy and updating apps for the latest features will enhance your experience. We'll cover tips for organizing your apps into folders, rearranging them to keep your favorites easily accessible, and deleting apps you no longer use to free up space. Keeping apps updated is also essential, as updates improve functionality, fix bugs, and enhance security. You'll learn how to enable automatic updates and manage updates manually if you prefer.

Finally, we'll look at some **recommended apps for seniors**, focusing on categories like health, hobbies, and entertainment. These apps can help you stay active, manage your wellness, learn new skills, and enjoy your leisure time. From step counters and meditation apps to games and hobby-focused tools, we'll introduce some top picks that may align with your interests, making it easier to explore new and helpful applications.

By the end of this chapter, you'll feel confident navigating the App Store, choosing apps that suit your needs, and keeping your iPhone organized and up-to-date. Let's dive in and explore how to unlock the full potential of your iPhone 16 through apps, making everyday tasks easier, more enjoyable, and enriching. Whether you're looking to simplify daily routines, stay connected with family, or explore new hobbies, there's an app for every need and interest, ready to add value to your day-to-day life.

Navigating the App Store and Downloading Apps

The App Store is your go-to destination for discovering, downloading, and updating apps that can enhance your iPhone experience. With apps for nearly every need—ranging from health and fitness to hobbies, entertainment, and productivity—the App Store offers a vast selection designed to help you personalize your device to fit your lifestyle. Navigating the App Store and finding high-quality apps that meet your interests can greatly expand your iPhone's usefulness. In this section, we'll cover how to browse, search, evaluate, and download apps from the App Store.

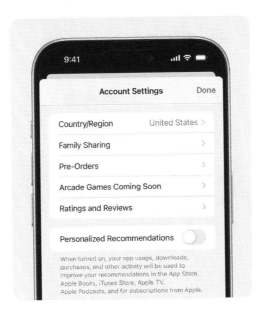

The App Store is pre-installed on your iPhone and can be accessed from your Home Screen:

- **Opening the App Store**: Tap the blue **App Store** icon with a white "A" on your Home Screen to open it. You'll be taken to the Today page, which showcases featured apps, collections, and articles curated by Apple.
- **Signing In with Apple ID**: To download apps, you need an Apple ID. If you haven't set one up, go to **Settings > [Your Name] > Media & Purchases** and tap **Sign In** or **Create Apple ID**. This account will be used for downloading apps, as well as making in-app purchases if you choose to do so.

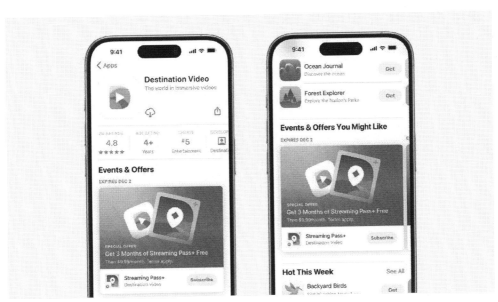

The App Store's interface is organized into several tabs at the bottom, each offering a different way to explore apps:

- **Today**: The Today tab highlights curated app suggestions, daily stories, and featured apps selected by Apple's editorial team. It's a great place to discover popular apps or learn about new releases and app updates.
- **Games**: Here, you'll find both free and paid games, from casual puzzles to immersive adventures. The Games tab also includes categories like "Top Free Games" and "Top Paid Games," making it easy to find popular options.
- **Apps**: The Apps tab includes categories like "Top Free Apps," "Top Paid Apps," and "Top Categories." This section covers everything outside of gaming, from fitness and cooking apps to finance and productivity tools.
- **Arcade**: Apple Arcade is a subscription-based service that offers unlimited access to a library of exclusive games. If you're interested in exploring new games without ads or in-app purchases, the Arcade tab is worth a look.

- **Search**: Use the Search tab to directly search for specific apps by name or keywords. This is helpful if you know the type of app you're looking for or if someone has recommended a specific app.

Each tab in the App Store offers a different way to find apps, giving you plenty of options for browsing and discovering what you need.

If you have a particular app in mind or are searching for apps that fall under a specific category, the **Search** tab is your best tool:

- **Using the Search Bar**:
  - » Tap the **Search** tab at the bottom of the App Store and enter keywords or the name of an app in the search bar. For example, you could search "health tracker," "photography editor," or "news apps."
  - » The search results will display a list of apps relevant to your query, along with icons, brief descriptions, ratings, and download buttons.
- **Exploring App Categories**:
  - » Under the Apps tab, you'll find a list of categories such as Health & Fitness, Entertainment, Finance, and Education. Tapping on a category shows a selection of related apps, making it easier to discover apps that align with specific interests.
  - » Categories are useful if you're not looking for a specific app but want to explore apps tailored to a particular activity or purpose.

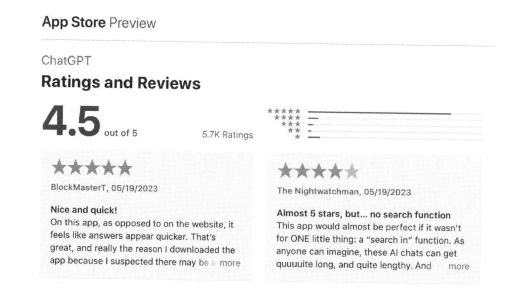

App Store Preview

ChatGPT
Ratings and Reviews

4.5 out of 5   5.7K Ratings

★★★★★

BlockMasterT, 05/19/2023

Nice and quick!
On this app, as opposed to on the website, it feels like answers appear quicker. That's great, and really the reason I downloaded the app because I suspected there may be a more

★★★★☆

The Nightwatchman, 05/19/2023

Almost 5 stars, but... no search function
This app would almost be perfect if it wasn't for ONE little thing: a "search in" function. As anyone can imagine, these AI chats can get quuuuite long, and quite lengthy. And   more

Before downloading an app, it's a good idea to evaluate its quality and usefulness. Here are some key factors to consider:

- **Reading Descriptions**:
  - » Tap on the app's icon in the search results to open its App Store page. Here, you'll see a description of the app's features, screenshots, compatibility information, and any updates. Reading the description helps you understand what the app does and how it might fit your needs.

- **Checking Ratings and Reviews**:
  - » Ratings are displayed on each app's page, along with an average star rating out of five. Reading reviews from other users can give you a sense of the app's performance, ease of use, and reliability. Look for apps with a high average rating and positive feedback for a better experience.
  - » Reviews are especially helpful if you're looking for specific features or want to know about any common issues users face.

- **Assessing In-App Purchases and Subscription Models**:
  - » Many apps are free to download but offer in-app purchases or subscription options for additional features. You'll find details about in-app purchases below the app description, marked as "Offers In-App Purchases."
  - » Some free apps also offer paid subscriptions for ad-free experiences or premium features. If an app is marked as free, be aware that some features may still require payment.

Once you've chosen an app, downloading it is easy:

- **Tapping the Download Button**:
  - » On the app's page, tap the **Get** button if it's free or the price button if it's paid. You may be prompted to confirm the download using **Face ID**, **Touch ID**, or your Apple ID password.
  - » After confirming, the app will begin downloading, and a progress circle will appear. Once the app has downloaded, it will be available on your Home Screen.

- **Managing Incomplete or Paused Downloads**:
  - » If you need to pause or cancel the download, you can do so by tapping on the app's icon on the Home Screen. Tapping it again resumes the download. Pausing downloads can be helpful if you're on a limited data plan or need to free up bandwidth temporarily.

Keeping your apps updated ensures you have access to the latest features, bug fixes, and security improvements. Here's how to manage app updates and settings:

- **Automatic Updates**:
  - » To enable automatic updates, go to **Settings > App Store** and toggle on **App Updates**. With this setting, your apps will update automatically whenever a new version is released, keeping them current without any extra effort.

- **Manual Updates**:
  - » You can also check for updates manually. Open the **App Store**, tap your **Profile Icon** at the top right, and scroll down to view available updates. Tap **Update** next to individual apps or select **Update All** to update all apps at once.

- **Re-downloading Purchased Apps**:
  - » If you've previously deleted a purchased app and want to re-download it, go to the **Purchased** section under your profile in the App Store. Here, you can see all apps linked to your Apple ID, allowing you to download them again without paying.

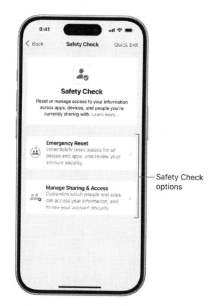

Safety Check options

Downloading apps from the App Store is generally safe, as Apple reviews each app before allowing it on the platform. However, taking some extra precautions ensures a secure experience:

- **Avoiding Suspicious Apps**:

- » Stick to apps with high ratings, a solid number of downloads, and positive reviews. Avoid apps with overly generic descriptions or poor ratings, as these may not be reliable.
- » Be cautious with apps that ask for unnecessary permissions. For instance, a calculator app shouldn't need access to your photos or location.

- **Reviewing App Permissions**:
  - » Once you download an app, it may ask for permissions, such as access to your camera, microphone, or location. You can control permissions by going to **Settings > Privacy** and reviewing each app's permissions to ensure they align with the app's functions.

If you're interested in exploring games, consider Apple Arcade—a subscription service that offers a selection of high-quality games without ads or in-app purchases:

- **Exploring Apple Arcade**:
  - » Open the App Store and tap the **Arcade** tab. You'll see a library of exclusive games across genres like puzzle, strategy, and adventure, all available through an Apple Arcade subscription.
  - » Apple Arcade is ideal for users who enjoy gaming without interruptions, as all games included in the subscription are ad-free.

- **Trying Out Apple Arcade**:
  - » Apple offers a free trial for Apple Arcade, allowing you to explore the service before committing. This can be a great way to sample a variety of games and see if they align with your preferences.

Navigating the App Store and downloading apps is a simple yet powerful way to expand your iPhone 16's capabilities. From exploring categories to finding specific tools that suit your lifestyle, the App Store has something for everyone. By evaluating app quality, managing downloads, and staying mindful of permissions, you'll be able to customize your iPhone with apps that enhance your day-to-day experience. Whether you're looking for entertainment, productivity, health tools, or ways to pursue hobbies, the App Store provides endless possibilities to enrich your iPhone experience.

Organizing, Deleting, and Updating Apps

Keeping your iPhone 16 organized and up-to-date enhances its functionality, helps you access apps quickly, and frees up storage space. With a range of features designed for customizing your Home Screen, arranging app folders, and keeping apps current, managing apps on your iPhone is easy and efficient. This section will guide you through organizing apps for better accessibility, deleting unused apps to optimize space, and updating apps to ensure you have the latest features and security improvements.

An organized Home Screen makes navigating your iPhone simpler, with your most-used apps always within easy reach. Here's how to arrange and customize your app layout:

- **Rearranging Apps**:
  - » To move apps around on your Home Screen, tap and hold an app icon until all the apps start to wiggle. Then, drag the app to a new position. You can move it to another spot on the same screen, or drag it to the edge of the screen to move it to another page.
  - » Rearranging your Home Screen so that your most-used apps are at the top or on the first screen helps you find them quickly, reducing the need to scroll.

- **Creating Folders for Similar Apps**:
  - » Organize apps by grouping them into folders based on categories, like "Social," "Work," "Games," or "Health." To create a folder, tap and hold an app until it starts to wiggle, then drag it on top of another app. This will automatically create a new folder.
  - » You can rename the folder by tapping the name field and typing a new title that reflects the contents. Organizing apps in folders reduces screen clutter and allows you to fit more apps onto a single page.

- **Using the App Library for Quick Access**:
  - » The App Library is located on the last page of your Home Screen and organizes all your apps automatically into categories like Productivity, Social, Entertainment, and Recently Added.
  - » To access the App Library, swipe left until you reach the last page. You can find any app by browsing categories or using the search bar at the top. The App Library is helpful for finding apps without scrolling through multiple Home Screen pages, and you can even remove less-used apps from the Home Screen, keeping them in the App Library for easy access.

Deleting unused apps is a simple way to free up storage space and reduce clutter. There are several ways to delete apps, depending on your preference:

- **Deleting Apps from the Home Screen**:
  - » Tap and hold an app icon until it starts wiggling, then tap the **Minus (-)** icon that appears in the top left corner of the app icon. Choose **Delete App** to confirm.
  - » You can also select **Remove from Home Screen** instead, which keeps the app in the App Library but removes it from the Home Screen. This option is helpful if you want to reduce clutter without permanently deleting the app.

- **Deleting Apps from the App Library**:
  - » In the App Library, press and hold an app icon, then tap **Delete App**. This action removes the app completely from your iPhone, freeing up storage.

- **Deleting Apps through Settings**:
  - » Go to **Settings > General > iPhone Storage**. Here, you'll see a list of all apps installed on your device, along with the amount of storage each one uses. Tap on an app to see more details and select **Delete App** if you want to remove it.
  - » Viewing apps by storage usage helps you identify which apps take up the most space, making it easy to delete large or rarely used apps.

- **Using Offload Unused Apps**:
  - » If you want to free up space without fully deleting apps, consider enabling **Offload Unused Apps** under **Settings > General > iPhone Storage**. This feature automatically removes apps you don't use often, but keeps their data so you can restore them easily.
  - » Offloading is especially useful for infrequently used apps that you may want to keep data for, like a travel app you use only occasionally. When you need the app again, simply tap on its icon, and it will re-download with all saved data intact.

Updating apps is essential for accessing the latest features, bug fixes, and security patches. Here's how to manage app updates on your iPhone 16:

- **Automatic App Updates**:

  » To enable automatic updates, go to **Settings > App Store** and toggle on **App Updates**. With this setting enabled, your iPhone will automatically download updates when they become available.

  » Automatic updates are convenient, as they ensure your apps stay current without requiring manual checks. However, if you prefer to control updates manually, you can turn off automatic updates and manage them yourself.

- **Manually Updating Apps**:

  » To check for updates manually, open the **App Store** and tap on your **Profile Icon** in the upper right corner. Scroll down to see a list of available updates. Tap **Update** next to individual apps, or select **Update All** to update all apps at once.

  » Manual updates allow you to choose which apps to update, which can be helpful if you want to avoid updating certain apps due to data usage or feature changes.

- **Viewing Update History**:

  » To see what has changed in recent updates, tap on the app's name in the update list within the App Store. Most apps include release notes detailing new features, improvements, or bug fixes. This information helps you stay informed about changes and improvements to your apps.

Keeping your apps organized and up-to-date is only part of app management. Here are a few extra tips to improve your app experience:

- **Using Widgets for Frequently Used Apps**:
  - » Widgets allow you to see app information directly on your Home Screen without opening the app. For example, a weather widget can show the forecast, while a calendar widget displays upcoming events.
  - » To add a widget, press and hold an empty space on the Home Screen, tap the **Plus (+)** icon in the top corner, select a widget, and choose its size. Widgets save you time by displaying key app information at a glance.

- **Customizing the Dock for Quick Access**:
  - » The Dock at the bottom of your Home Screen can hold up to four apps, making it ideal for your most-used applications, such as Phone, Messages, Safari, or Mail. Drag an app to or from the Dock while in editing mode to customize it.
  - » Keeping essential apps in the Dock provides quick access from any Home Screen page, making it easier to reach your favorite apps.

- **Utilizing Spotlight Search for Fast Access**:
  - » If you have many apps or frequently switch between them, Spotlight Search is a quick way to find any app on your iPhone. Swipe down on any Home Screen to open Spotlight, then type the app's name in the search bar.
  - » Spotlight is faster than scrolling and can be especially helpful for finding apps you don't keep on your Home Screen or for finding content within apps.

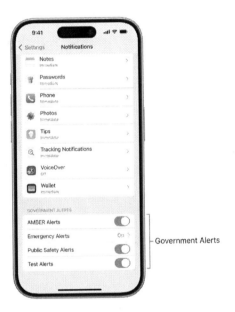

Too many notifications can be overwhelming, but managing them effectively keeps you informed without unnecessary distractions:

- **Customizing Notifications for Each App**:
  - » Go to **Settings > Notifications** to adjust notifications for individual apps. You can choose to allow notifications, turn them off entirely, or customize how they appear (e.g., sound, banners, or badges).
  - » Adjusting notifications helps you prioritize important apps and reduce interruptions from less critical ones, creating a more focused app experience.

- **Using Scheduled Summary**:
  - » Scheduled Summary groups less-important notifications and delivers them at a specific time, reducing interruptions. Enable this feature in **Settings > Notifications > Scheduled Summary** to consolidate alerts from apps you don't need immediate updates from.
  - » This feature is especially helpful for organizing notifications from social media or shopping apps, allowing you to check them at a convenient time rather than receiving constant notifications.

Backing up your apps and data ensures that your information is safe in case you switch devices or need to restore your iPhone:

- **Using iCloud Backup**:
  - » iCloud automatically backs up your app data when iCloud Backup is enabled. Go to **Settings > [Your Name] > iCloud > iCloud Backup** and toggle it on. This feature saves app data, settings, and other important information.
  - » With iCloud Backup, you can restore your apps and data easily if you get a new iPhone or need to reset your current one.
- **Backing Up Locally with iTunes or Finder**:
  - » If you prefer a local backup, connect your iPhone to a computer and use iTunes (on Windows) or Finder (on Mac) to create a complete backup of your device. This includes apps, settings, and media, and can be restored if needed.
  - » Local backups offer a complete snapshot of your device and are ideal for people who want control over their data without relying on cloud storage.

Organizing, deleting, and updating apps on your iPhone 16 helps keep your device running smoothly and tailored to your needs. By arranging your Home Screen, using folders, and taking advantage of the App Library, you can create a tidy and efficient setup that makes it easy to find apps and focus on what's important. Deleting unused apps frees up valuable storage, while regular updates keep your apps performing well with the latest features and security improvements. With these tools and techniques, your iPhone can stay organized, secure, and optimized for a personalized experience.

Recommended Apps for Seniors (Health, Hobbies, Entertainment)

Your iPhone 16 opens up a world of opportunities to improve your daily life, pursue hobbies, stay healthy, and stay entertained—all through a range of apps designed with simplicity, ease of use, and accessibility in mind. In this section, we'll explore some of the best apps for seniors across three key categories: health, hobbies, and entertainment. These apps are user-friendly, practical, and tailored to help you live a more connected, healthy, and enjoyable life.

1. Health Apps

Staying on top of health is crucial, and there are several apps that can help with fitness, medication management, and mindfulness, making it easier to take care of your well-being.

- **Apple Health** (Free):
  - » Apple Health is a built-in app that provides a comprehensive look at your health data, including activity levels, sleep, and more. If you have an Apple Watch, it syncs seamlessly to track daily steps, heart rate, and exercise goals. The app also includes a "Health Checklist" feature that lets you manage health records, emergency contacts, and important medical information like allergies and medications.

- » Apple Health organizes data in an easy-to-navigate interface, making it ideal for tracking progress and staying motivated with your health goals.

- **Medisafe** (Free, with in-app purchases):
  - » Medisafe is a medication management app designed to help you remember to take your prescriptions on time. The app provides reminders for each medication, detailed information about your medications, and refill alerts. Medisafe also allows you to add family members who can monitor your schedule, helping ensure you stay on track.
  - » It's an excellent app for those managing multiple medications, as it offers a clear, customizable schedule that's easy to follow.

- **MyFitnessPal** (Free, with premium option):
  - » MyFitnessPal helps you monitor your nutrition and fitness, with an extensive database for tracking meals, calories, and physical activity. You can set personalized health goals, and the app offers guidance on making healthier food choices.
  - » MyFitnessPal's intuitive interface and daily tracking make it easy to use, helping you stay mindful of your diet and overall wellness. The app also offers a social component if you'd like to join groups for motivation.

- **Calm** (Free, with premium option):
  - » Calm is a mindfulness and meditation app that offers guided sessions for stress relief, sleep, and focus. With features like breathing exercises, sleep stories, and relaxing sounds, Calm is perfect for those looking to reduce anxiety and improve sleep quality.
  - » The app's user-friendly design and wide variety of relaxation options make it easy to incorporate meditation into daily routines, providing tools for both beginners and those familiar with mindfulness.

Whether you enjoy reading, gardening, cooking, or exploring new skills, there are apps to help you pursue your hobbies and discover new interests.

- **Libby, by Over Drive** (Free):
  - » Libby is a digital library app that connects with your local library, allowing you to borrow e-books and audiobooks for free. With thousands of titles available across genres, Libby provides an excellent way to enjoy books without needing to visit a physical library.
  - » Libby's reading-friendly interface, adjustable font sizes, and audiobook options make it accessible for everyone. It's perfect for book lovers or anyone looking to explore new reading material on the go.

- **Garden Answers** (Free, with in-app purchases):
  - » Garden Answers is a plant identification app that helps you identify flowers, plants, and trees by simply taking a

photo. The app provides care tips, growing information, and troubleshooting advice, making it an ideal tool for both beginner and experienced gardeners.

  » With its large plant database and easy-to-use photo identification feature, Garden Answers is especially helpful for those who enjoy gardening or want to learn more about plants in their surroundings.

- **Tasty** (Free):

  » Tasty is a cooking app that offers thousands of easy-to-follow recipes with step-by-step instructions and instructional videos. You can filter recipes by dietary preferences, cooking time, and difficulty level, making it easy to find meals that fit your needs.

  » Tasty's video tutorials are particularly useful for trying new recipes, and the app's search features make it easy to find recipes for any occasion. It's a great resource for cooking enthusiasts or anyone looking to improve their kitchen skills.

- **Duolingo** (Free, with premium option):

  » Duolingo is a language-learning app that makes it fun and easy to learn new languages. With interactive lessons and games, you can practice languages like Spanish, French, German, and many others at your own pace.

  » Duolingo's short, gamified lessons and encouraging notifications make it suitable for beginners and those looking to improve language skills. It's an excellent tool for learning new languages or keeping the brain active with daily language exercises.

Entertainment apps are a great way to enjoy free time, from streaming movies and music to playing games. Here are some top entertainment apps that are accessible and offer a wide range of content.

- **Netflix** (Subscription required):

  » Netflix is one of the most popular streaming platforms, offering thousands of movies, TV shows, and documentaries. With options to watch offline and a variety of genres, Netflix provides endless entertainment for all tastes.

  » The app's user-friendly interface and personalized recommendations make it easy to find content you'll enjoy. Netflix is perfect for unwinding with a movie, discovering new shows, or exploring interesting documentaries.

- **Spotify** (Free with ads, or subscription required for premium):

  » Spotify is a music streaming app that provides access to millions of songs, playlists, and podcasts. With a variety of curated playlists and personalized recommendations, you can find music for every mood or discover new artists.

  » Spotify's vast library and easy-to-navigate design make it a top choice for music lovers. The free version includes ads, but the premium version offers an ad-free experience and offline downloads.

- **Words with Friends** (Free, with in-app purchases):

  » Words with Friends is a popular word game app that allows you to play a Scrabble-like game with friends, family, or other players worldwide. It's an engaging way to exercise your mind, expand your vocabulary, and stay connected with loved ones.

» With options to play against random opponents or connect with friends, Words with Friends is perfect for those who enjoy word games and friendly competition.

- **YouTube** (Free, with subscription option for YouTube Premium):
  » YouTube is the world's largest video-sharing platform, where you can watch content on virtually any topic—from cooking tutorials to travel guides, music videos, and more. You can also follow channels that align with your interests.
  » YouTube is a versatile app for entertainment, learning, and exploring new interests. For a more immersive experience, YouTube Premium offers ad-free content, offline downloads, and background play.
- **Lumosity** (Free, with subscription option):
  » Lumosity is a brain-training app that provides a series of fun games designed to improve memory, focus, and problem-solving skills. With daily exercises and challenges, Lumosity offers a way to keep your mind sharp and engaged.
  » Lumosity's interactive games and tracking features make it easy to measure progress and stay motivated. It's a great app for maintaining cognitive health and enjoying short, engaging exercises.

Tips for Finding and Using Apps

- **Reading Reviews and Checking Ratings**: Before downloading an app, check its reviews and ratings on the App Store. Positive reviews and a high rating indicate a well-made app that other users have found helpful and reliable.
- **Exploring Free Trials and Subscriptions**: Some apps offer free trials or have premium versions with additional features. Taking advantage of free trials lets you test the app's functionality before committing to a subscription.
- **Customizing Notifications**: For apps that send regular updates or notifications, customize the notification settings in your iPhone's settings to reduce interruptions and only receive relevant alerts.

With the right apps, your iPhone 16 can become a personalized hub for health management, hobbies, and entertainment, enhancing your daily life in meaningful ways. From tracking fitness and medications to enjoying books, learning new skills, and staying entertained, these recommended apps cater to various interests and needs. By incorporating these apps into your routine, you'll find that your iPhone can help you stay active, engaged, and entertained every day, supporting a balanced and fulfilling lifestyle.

CHAPTER 9
PHOTOS & VIDEOS

Welcome to Chapter 9: Photos & Videos! Your iPhone 16 is equipped with an impressive camera and a range of tools that make capturing, editing, and sharing moments easy and enjoyable. From stunning sunsets to spontaneous family gatherings, you have everything you need to document life's memorable moments right in your pocket. In this chapter, we'll explore essential tips for using your iPhone's camera effectively, editing your photos and videos to bring out their best, and organizing and sharing them effortlessly with family and friends.

We'll start with **camera tips and photography basics**, where you'll learn to make the most of your iPhone's powerful camera. From adjusting focus and exposure to using features like Portrait mode, Night mode, and the zoom lens, these tips will help you take high-quality photos that capture moments beautifully. You'll also learn about composing shots, finding good lighting, and using simple techniques that can turn any snapshot into a memorable photograph.

Next, we'll dive into **editing photos and videos on your iPhone**. The Photos app offers a range of easy-to-use editing tools that allow you to enhance colors, adjust brightness, crop, add filters, and more—all without needing a separate app. Editing allows you to refine your images and videos to make them look polished and professional. We'll go through each editing tool step-by-step, helping you learn how to make simple adjustments that can bring out the best in every shot.

Finally, we'll cover **creating albums and sharing with family**. Organizing your photos into albums makes it easy to find specific memories and keep track of important events, like vacations, holidays, or birthdays. You'll learn how to create and label albums, as well as how to share them privately with family members or friends using iCloud. This feature is perfect for staying connected and sharing special moments, even when you're not in the same place.

By the end of this chapter, you'll have a solid foundation for capturing high-quality photos and videos, editing them to highlight their best qualities, and sharing them with those who matter most. Your iPhone's camera and editing tools are designed to make photography accessible and enjoyable, regardless of experience level. So, let's explore how to make your memories look their best and bring out the joy of capturing life's precious moments with your iPhone 16!

Camera Tips and Photography Basics

The iPhone 16 camera is a powerful tool for capturing life's moments, from family gatherings to breathtaking landscapes. With its advanced features, taking high-quality photos and videos is accessible to everyone, regardless of photography experience. In this section, we'll cover the basics of photography on your iPhone, including essential tips and techniques that will help you take clear, beautiful images. By learning how to use features like focus, exposure, and composition, you can turn ordinary snapshots into memorable photos.

Understanding the camera interface is the first step to capturing great photos:

- **Opening the Camera**: Open the Camera app by tapping the camera icon on the Home Screen or swiping left from the Lock Screen. This quick access ensures you never miss a moment.
- **Navigating Camera Modes**: At the bottom of the screen, you'll find various camera modes, including **Photo, Portrait, Video**, **Slo-Mo, Time-Lapse, Pano**, and **Cinematic**. Swipe left or right to switch between modes depending on your shooting goals. The **Photo** mode is best for general photography, while **Portrait** adds a professional blur effect to the background, perfect for capturing people.
- **Zoom Options**: The iPhone 16 features multiple lenses, including wide, ultra-wide, and telephoto. Tap the **1x, 0.5x,** or **3x** icons to switch between zoom levels, or use the pinch-to-zoom gesture to adjust the zoom smoothly. Each lens offers a unique perspective, allowing you to capture more detail or get a wider view.

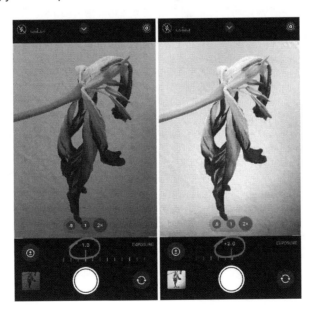

The iPhone camera automatically focuses and adjusts exposure, but you can manually control these settings to achieve more precise results:

- **Setting Focus**:

» Tap on your subject on the screen to lock focus. You'll see a yellow box appear, indicating the focal point. This ensures your subject remains sharp, even if you move the camera slightly.
» For photos with multiple subjects, tap on the one you want to emphasize, and your iPhone will adjust focus accordingly. This feature is useful for capturing detailed portraits, close-ups of flowers, or pets.

• **Adjusting Exposure**:
» Once you set the focus, you'll see a small sun icon next to the focus box. Slide the sun icon up or down to increase or decrease the exposure. Lowering exposure can add richness to colors, while increasing it brightens the image.
» Experiment with exposure settings to achieve the right balance of light, especially in challenging lighting situations like bright sunlight or low-light interiors.

Portrait mode is a powerful feature that adds a beautiful depth-of-field effect, making the subject stand out by blurring the background:

• **Activating Portrait Mode**:
» Swipe to **Portrait** mode in the Camera app. The camera will prompt you to move closer or farther from your subject for the best results.
» Portrait mode works best for capturing people but also works beautifully for pets, flowers, or objects. This mode can make simple shots look like they were taken by a professional.

• **Adjusting Background Blur**:
» After taking a portrait photo, you can adjust the level of background blur by tapping **Edit** on the photo, selecting **f** (aperture) at the top, and moving the slider. Lower aperture values increase the blur, while higher values keep more of the background in focus.
» Experiment with different levels of blur to find the perfect balance. Subtle adjustments can add depth and draw the viewer's eye to the main subject.

Night mode enhances photos taken in dim lighting, preserving detail and color while reducing noise:

- **Activating Night Mode**:
  - » When the iPhone detects low light, Night mode activates automatically. You'll see a yellow **Night Mode** icon at the top of the screen, along with a number indicating the exposure time in seconds.
  - » Hold your iPhone steady or use a tripod to minimize motion during exposure. Night mode will capture several frames over a few seconds, combining them for a clear, well-lit result.

- **Adjusting Exposure Time**:
  - » Tap the Night mode icon to adjust the exposure time, which is typically between 1–10 seconds, depending on the lighting. Longer exposures capture more light but require a very steady hand or a tripod.
  - » Night mode is ideal for evening landscapes, city lights, and capturing details indoors without flash. Experiment with exposure times to find the best settings for each scene.

Composition plays a significant role in making photos visually appealing. Here are some composition basics to enhance your photos:

- **The Rule of Thirds**:

- » The rule of thirds is a fundamental principle in photography. Imagine your screen divided into a 3x3 grid. Place your subject along one of these lines or at the intersections for a balanced, dynamic composition.
- » To enable the grid, go to **Settings > Camera** and toggle on **Grid**. Using the grid can help you create visually engaging photos by positioning subjects off-center.

- **Leading Lines**:
  - » Leading lines are natural lines in a scene that guide the viewer's eye toward the subject. Roads, pathways, fences, or even a row of trees can serve as leading lines to draw focus.
  - » Look for leading lines in your environment to add depth and direct attention to your subject, giving your photos a more professional touch.

- **Framing**:
  - » Use elements in your surroundings to "frame" your subject, such as windows, doorways, or trees. Framing adds context and depth to your photos, making the subject stand out.
  - » Look for natural frames in your environment to add an artistic element to your photos, especially for portraits or architectural shots.

Motion can add a dynamic feel to photos, and your iPhone offers features to capture movement effectively:

- **Using Burst Mode**:
  - » Burst mode captures a series of photos in quick succession, perfect for capturing action shots. To use burst mode, press and hold the shutter button, and your iPhone will take multiple images in rapid sequence.
  - » Burst mode is ideal for capturing children, pets, or sports, where movement is unpredictable. You can review the burst series afterward and choose the best shots.

- **Live Photos for Moments in Motion**:
  - » Live Photos captures a few seconds of video around each photo, adding a touch of movement and sound. To activate, tap the **Live Photo** icon (circle with concentric rings) in the Camera app.
  - » Live Photos are great for capturing moments with subtle movement, like a laugh or a wave. You can play back Live Photos by pressing and holding the photo in your gallery.

HDR (High Dynamic Range) captures multiple exposures in a single shot, combining them for better detail in high-contrast scenes:

- **Activating HDR**:
  - » HDR is enabled automatically in most iPhone 16 settings, but you can manually turn it on or off by tapping the **HDR** icon in the Camera app.
  - » HDR is useful for scenes with a wide range of brightness, like landscapes with a bright sky and a darker foreground. It balances exposure across the image, preserving details in both bright and dark areas.

- **When to Use HDR**:
  - » Use HDR in situations where lighting contrast is extreme, like sunsets, shadows, or backlit scenes. Avoid HDR in very low light, as it may produce noise in darker areas.

The best way to improve your photography is to experiment with different features and techniques:

- **Practice in Different Lighting**:
  - » Test your iPhone's camera in various lighting situations—indoors, outdoors, morning, and evening—to understand how lighting impacts your photos. Pay attention to how Night mode, HDR, and exposure adjustments affect the final result.

- **Experiment with Angles**:

» Don't be afraid to change your perspective. Try taking photos from high or low angles, close-ups, and wide shots to add variety. Unique angles can make photos more interesting and help capture scenes from fresh perspectives.

- **Review and Edit**:
  » After shooting, review your photos and experiment with minor edits in the Photos app. Simple adjustments like cropping, increasing brightness, or applying a filter can make a big difference in the final look.

By mastering these basics of iPhone photography, you'll be equipped to capture beautiful, memorable photos with confidence. From learning how to adjust focus and exposure to experimenting with Portrait mode, Night mode, and creative composition, these tips will help you make the most of your iPhone 16 camera. As you continue to practice and experiment, your photos will reflect the moments you cherish, captured with clarity and style.

Editing Photos and Videos on Your iPhone

Editing photos and videos on your iPhone 16 is an intuitive process that can dramatically enhance the quality of your images. The built-in Photos app provides a wide range of tools that allow you to adjust colors, brightness, contrast, crop, apply filters, and more. Whether you're refining a snapshot or creating a polished video, these tools give you the ability to transform your photos and videos into visually striking memories. In this section, we'll go over each editing tool step-by-step, covering everything from basic adjustments to advanced effects that can take your photos and videos to the next level.

The Photos app is pre-installed on your iPhone, and accessing editing tools is as simple as selecting a photo or video:

- **Opening the Photos App**: Launch the **Photos** app from your Home Screen. Select the photo or video you want to edit, then tap **Edit** in the upper-right corner to enter editing mode.
- **Editing Interface**: Once in editing mode, you'll see three main sections for photos: **Adjustments**, **Filters**, and **Crop**. Each section offers specific tools for different types of edits. Videos will have similar tools, with additional options like trimming and adjusting playback speed.

The Adjustments section offers the essential tools for fine-tuning your photos. These adjustments help you enhance brightness, contrast, sharpness, and other visual aspects to make your photos stand out.

- **Auto-Enhance**:
  » The Auto-Enhance tool (a magic wand icon) applies a set of basic adjustments automatically, optimizing brightness, contrast, and color. Tap **Auto** to see immediate improvements to your photo, and make further adjustments if desired.

- **Exposure, Brightness, and Contrast**:
  » **Exposure** controls the overall light in the photo. Increasing exposure brightens the image, while decreasing it darkens it. Exposure adjustments are useful for photos taken in low or high light.
  » **Brightness** specifically enhances the light in mid-tones, making the image look naturally brighter or darker without affecting highlights and shadows too much.
  » **Contrast** adjusts the difference between light and dark areas. Increasing contrast can make colors pop and add drama, while decreasing it softens the overall look.
  » Experiment with exposure, brightness, and contrast to create the right balance, bringing out details and setting the mood of the photo.

- **Shadows and Highlights**:
  » **Highlights** control the brightest parts of the photo, helping to restore detail in overexposed areas.
  » **Shadows** adjust the darker areas, revealing hidden details in shaded parts of the image. Increasing shadows can brighten dark areas, while decreasing them adds depth.
  » Adjusting highlights and shadows can bring out textures and add depth to images with contrasting light sources, like sunset scenes or high-contrast portraits.

- **Sharpness and Definition**:

» **Sharpness** enhances fine details, making the image crisper. Use sharpness sparingly to avoid making the image look unnatural.
» **Definition** enhances edges in the image, adding clarity without introducing grain. This tool is ideal for portraits and landscapes, as it highlights textures in a natural way.

For more nuanced edits, the Photos app offers additional tools that allow you to customize the look of your photos even further:

* **Saturation, Vibrance, and Warmth**:
  » **Saturation** increases the intensity of all colors in the image. Be careful not to over-saturate, as this can make colors appear artificial.
  » **Vibrance** selectively enhances less intense colors, creating a balanced and natural effect that works well for portraits and landscapes.
  » **Warmth** adjusts the color temperature, making the image appear warmer (yellow/orange tones) or cooler (blue tones). Warmer tones add a sunny, inviting look, while cooler tones create a calm, moody effect.

* **Tint and Color Adjustments**:
  » **Tint** allows you to add subtle color shifts to balance out greens or reds in the image, particularly helpful for skin tones and landscapes.
  » Experiment with Tint alongside Saturation and Warmth to achieve the desired color tone.

* **Vignette**:
  » The Vignette tool darkens or lightens the edges of the photo, drawing attention to the center. A subtle vignette can help frame the subject and add focus to the image.
  » Adjusting the vignette effect is especially effective for portraits, where you want the viewer's attention to be on the subject's face.

* **Noise Reduction**:
  » Noise Reduction reduces the graininess or "noise" in low-light photos. While it can soften an image slightly, it's useful for cleaning up night or low-light shots, resulting in a smoother, clearer appearance.

Editing videos on your iPhone is just as simple as editing photos, with options to trim, adjust colors, and even control playback speed:

- **Trimming Clips**:
  - » Open the video in the Photos app, tap **Edit**, and use the sliders at the beginning and end of the timeline to trim unwanted parts. Trimming is helpful for removing unnecessary footage and focusing on the key moments.
  - » After adjusting, tap **Done** to save your trimmed video. The original video remains intact in case you want to re-edit.

- **Adjusting Brightness, Contrast, and Color**:
  - » Similar to photos, you can adjust a video's brightness, contrast, exposure, and color using the same tools. These adjustments are useful for enhancing the overall look of your video, especially if it was shot in poor lighting.
  - » For a cohesive look, use adjustments sparingly and review playback to ensure that the changes maintain the quality and flow of the footage.

- **Adding Filters**:
  - » Filters allow you to apply an overall style to the video, such as a vintage look, vivid colors, or a black-and-white effect. Filters are a great way to add mood or artistic flair to your videos.
  - » Experiment with different filters, but ensure that the effect aligns with the story or tone of the video.

- **Adjusting Playback Speed**:
  - » In the Photos app, you can't directly adjust video speed, but you can do so in the **iMovie** app, which is free on the App Store. iMovie allows you to speed up or slow down clips, add transitions, and create polished videos with additional editing features.

Filters provide a one-tap way to apply a stylistic effect to photos and videos, making it easy to enhance images quickly:

- **Applying Filters**:

    » Tap **Filters** in the Photos app and swipe through the options to preview each one. Filters like **Vivid**, **Warm**, **Cool**, **Mono** (black and white), and **Dramatic** offer instant style choices.

    » You can adjust the filter's intensity by moving the slider, allowing for subtle or bold effects. Filters are perfect for adding mood to your photos, such as brightening up a sunny beach photo or adding drama to a landscape.

- **Customizing Filter Strength**:

    » Instead of applying a filter at full strength, reduce the intensity for a more subtle effect. Lowering the filter strength allows the original colors and tones to come through while still adding a touch of style.

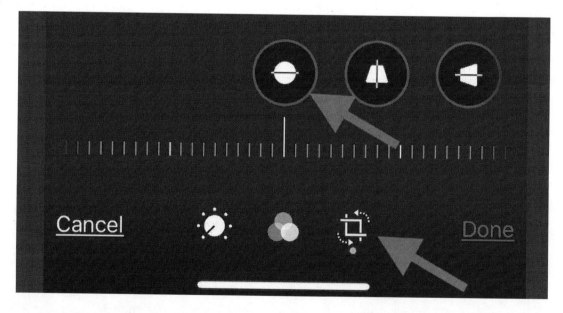

The Crop tool is essential for fine-tuning the composition and alignment of your photos:

- **Cropping**:

    » Use the Crop tool to remove unwanted areas and improve composition. Select **Aspect** to choose a preset ratio (such as Square, 4:3, or 16:9), or drag the corners of the crop box to create a custom frame.

    » Cropping can eliminate distractions at the edges, bringing more focus to your subject.

- **Straightening and Rotating**:

» If your photo is slightly tilted, use the **Straighten** tool to level it. The tool includes a grid overlay to help you align the photo perfectly. You can also rotate the image to change orientation from portrait to landscape, or vice versa.

» Straightening and rotating give you precise control over your photo's orientation, ensuring that each image is well-aligned and centered.

7. Saving and Reverting Edits

After editing, the Photos app saves a new version of your image or video while preserving the original. Here's how to manage your edits:

- **Saving Changes**:
  » When you're satisfied with your edits, tap **Done** to save them. The edited version will replace the original in your library, but you can always revert to the original later.

- **Reverting to the Original**:
  » To revert to the unedited version, open the photo or video, tap **Edit**, and then select **Revert**. This action will discard all edits, restoring the original file. This option gives you the freedom to experiment without worrying about permanently altering your images.

Editing photos and videos on your iPhone allows you to bring out the best in each image, capturing the essence of special moments with polished quality. Whether you're making simple adjustments, adding creative filters, or refining the composition, these tools help you transform everyday photos and videos into professional-looking memories. With practice and experimentation, you'll become confident in your editing skills, creating a personalized collection of memories that reflect your style and creativity.

Creating Albums and Sharing with Family

Creating albums and sharing photos and videos with family is a wonderful way to stay connected and organized. The Photos app on the iPhone 16 makes it easy to organize your memories into albums and securely share them with loved ones, allowing everyone to stay updated on special moments even when miles apart. In this section, we'll walk you through creating albums, organizing your photo collection, and using iCloud sharing features to share albums with family and friends. Whether it's holiday photos, family events, or daily moments, this guide will help you manage and share your visual memories effortlessly.

Albums are essential for organizing your photos and videos, making it easy to find specific memories or create collections based on themes or events:

- **Starting a New Album**:

» Open the **Photos** app, go to the **Albums** tab, and tap the **Plus (+)** icon in the top-left corner. Select **New Album** and enter a name for your album, such as "Family Vacation 2023" or "Grandkids."

» After naming your album, select the photos and videos you want to include. Tap **Done** to create the album, which will now appear under **My Albums** in the Albums tab.

- **Adding Photos to an Existing Album**:

  » To add more photos to an album later, select the photos you'd like to add, tap the **Share** icon, and select **Add to Album**. Choose the album you'd like to add them to, and they'll be included instantly.

  » Albums help keep your photos organized by theme, making it easier to navigate and share memories with specific groups of images.

- **Creating Smart Albums for Specific Categories**:

  » The Photos app automatically organizes certain types of photos into smart albums, such as **Favorites**, **People**, and **Places**. You can tag people and locations to organize your albums further, creating easy ways to view specific types of photos or locate moments tied to specific events.

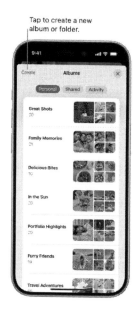

Tap to create a new album or folder.

Albums provide flexibility for grouping photos, allowing you to structure your collection in a way that makes sense for your lifestyle and preferences:

- **Using Favorites to Highlight Key Moments**:

  » Tap the **Heart** icon on any photo or video to mark it as a favorite, automatically adding it to your **Favorites** album. This album gathers all your favorite images in one place, making it easy to revisit cherished moments without searching.

  » Favorites is an excellent way to highlight the best moments from an event or keep track of photos you want to share with family later.

- **Organizing Albums by Date, Event, or Theme**:

  » Consider creating albums for each event, such as "Birthday 2023," "Christmas," or "Graduation." Alternatively, organize photos by themes, like "Nature Walks" or "Recipes."

  » Creating themed or event-specific albums allows you to quickly find and share specific moments, especially if you have a large photo library.

- **Rearranging Albums for Easy Access**:

  » To rearrange albums, go to the **Albums** tab, tap **Edit**, then drag albums to reorder them. You can place frequently accessed albums near the top, saving time when navigating your collection.

  » Organizing albums in a way that suits your routine ensures that you can always find what you need, quickly and easily.

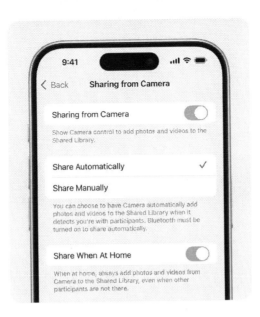

Shared Albums are a fantastic way to share photos and videos privately with family and friends. They allow everyone to contribute to an album, so each member can add their own photos and leave comments. Here's how to set up and manage shared albums:

- **Creating a Shared Album**:
  - » In the Photos app, go to **Albums**, tap the **Plus (+)** icon, and select **New Shared Album**. Give the album a name, such as "Family Reunion 2023," then invite family members by entering their Apple IDs or email addresses.
  - » Once created, everyone in the group can view, comment on, and add photos to the shared album, making it a collaborative memory book for events and milestones.

- **Inviting Family and Friends**:
  - » After setting up a shared album, tap **People** in the album settings and add family members you want to invite. If they're using an iPhone, iPad, or Mac, they'll receive an invitation to join the album in their Photos app.
  - » Sharing albums through iCloud is secure and private, ensuring that only invited participants can view and contribute to the album.

- **Adding Photos and Comments**:
  - » To add photos, open the shared album, tap **Add**, and select images from your library. Everyone in the album will see new photos as they're added.
  - » You and other members can also leave comments on individual photos, adding a personal touch to the shared album. Commenting on shared photos is a fun way to interact with family, especially for long-distance relatives who may not see these moments in person.

 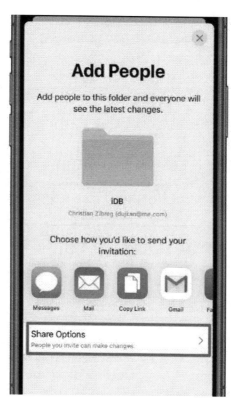 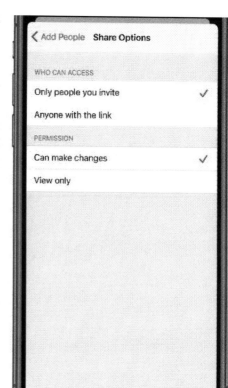

iCloud provides convenient and secure options for sharing your albums with family, whether they have an Apple device or not. Here's how to get the most out of iCloud's sharing features:

- **Shared Albums with iCloud**:
  - » Shared Albums allow you to invite family members to view, comment on, and add to albums. This feature is useful for creating family photo libraries that everyone can access from their own devices.
  - » Shared Albums don't take up iCloud storage, making it an ideal option for large family collections.

- **Enabling iCloud Photos for Automatic Sharing**:
  - » Enabling **iCloud Photos** automatically uploads and syncs your entire photo library across all your Apple devices. This ensures that any new photos or videos you take are instantly available on your other devices, and it also backs up your entire library securely in iCloud.
  - » Go to **Settings > [Your Name] > iCloud > Photos** and toggle on **iCloud Photos**. This feature is especially useful if you take a lot of photos and want access to them anytime, anywhere.

- **Creating Public Web Links for Non-Apple Users**:
  - » If you want to share an album with family members who don't use Apple devices, you can create a public link. In the shared album, go to **People** settings and toggle on **Public Website**. This generates a URL that you can share with anyone, even if they don't have an Apple ID.
  - » This link allows non-Apple users to view the album from any web browser, making it easy to share memories with everyone, regardless of their device.

Shared albums can grow quickly, especially when multiple family members contribute. Here's how to manage and organize shared albums effectively:

- **Deleting or Removing Photos from Shared Albums**:
  - » If you want to remove a photo from a shared album, open the album, tap **Select**, choose the photo, and tap **Delete**. This removes the photo from the album for everyone, so use this feature carefully.
  - » As the album creator, you have control over the content, so you can manage the album to keep it organized and relevant.

- **Setting Notifications for Shared Albums**:
  - » To receive alerts when new photos or comments are added to shared albums, enable notifications in **Settings > Notifications > Photos > Shared Album Activity**. Notifications keep you updated on new additions, making it easy to stay engaged with shared albums.
  - » Notifications are helpful for large family albums where new photos or comments are added frequently, ensuring you don't miss any updates.

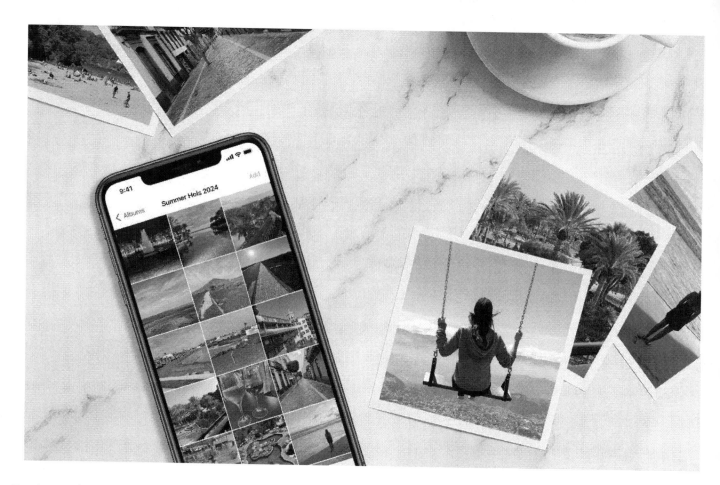

For those who enjoy printed photo albums, Apple offers the option to create and order photo books, prints, and other physical keepsakes through third-party services integrated within the Photos app. Here's how to preserve memories as physical albums:

- **Ordering Prints and Albums**:
  - » Select photos from an album, tap the **Share** icon, and look for printing options or third-party apps that let you order physical albums, photo books, or prints.
  - » Printed albums make wonderful gifts for family members and provide a physical collection of memories that can be cherished for years.

- **Creating Themed Albums for Special Occasions**:
  - » Consider creating albums dedicated to specific occasions, like "2023 Family Holiday" or "Grandkids' Milestones." These themed albums can be printed as gifts or keepsakes, providing a lasting way to celebrate family moments.
  - » Printed albums are perfect for family members who may prefer physical photos over digital ones, offering a thoughtful way to share memories.

Organizing photos and sharing them with family through albums brings everyone closer, allowing you to relive and celebrate special moments together. With iCloud's Shared Albums, creating and managing collections of memories is easy, collaborative, and secure. Whether you're organizing photos by event, sharing albums with loved ones, or ordering physical prints, these tools allow you to preserve and enjoy your memories for years to come. By mastering these features, you can turn your iPhone 16 into a central hub for family memories, making each photo a treasured part of your shared history.

CHAPTER 10
APPLE PAY & WALLET

Welcome to Chapter 10: Apple Pay & Wallet! The iPhone 16's Wallet app, paired with Apple Pay, offers a convenient, secure, and efficient way to manage payments and store essential items like credit cards, boarding passes, and more. With these tools, you can make purchases both in stores and online, track transactions, and keep your payment information safe—all without needing to carry a physical wallet. This chapter will guide you through setting up Apple Pay, making secure payments, and managing your digital wallet to maximize convenience and security.

We'll start by discussing **setting up Apple Pay and the Digital Wallet**, a straightforward process that takes only a few minutes. By adding your payment cards to Apple Pay, you'll have a digital wallet that allows you to make purchases with a quick tap. Whether you're paying at a store, shopping online, or even purchasing within an app, Apple Pay simplifies transactions and keeps your card details secure.

Next, we'll cover **making payments securely** with Apple Pay. One of the standout features of Apple Pay is its emphasis on security, which uses technology like Face ID, Touch ID, and unique transaction codes to protect your information. Each transaction is private, with no card numbers exchanged, reducing the risk of theft or fraud. You'll learn how to make payments with confidence, knowing that your information is safeguarded at every step.

Finally, we'll go over **tips for managing payment information** in your Wallet. Keeping your digital wallet organized, managing multiple cards, and understanding Apple Pay's privacy features can make your experience smoother and more efficient. You'll learn how to update card details, monitor transactions, and securely manage your payment methods for peace of mind.

By the end of this chapter, you'll have a thorough understanding of how to use Apple Pay and the Wallet app to streamline your financial interactions, protect your payment information, and enjoy the convenience of a digital wallet. With Apple Pay and Wallet on your iPhone 16, everyday transactions become faster, safer, and more efficient, making it easy to embrace a cash-free and card-free lifestyle. Let's dive in and explore how to get the most out of Apple Pay and Wallet, transforming the way you manage payments in today's digital world.

Setting Up Apple Pay and Digital Wallet

Setting up Apple Pay and the Wallet app on your iPhone 16 is a simple process that gives you access to a secure, contactless payment method and a convenient way to manage various digital cards. Once set up, Apple Pay allows you to make purchases with a tap or glance, whether you're shopping in-store, online, or within apps. This section will walk you through the steps to set up Apple Pay and your digital wallet, helping you get started on a path toward simplified and secure transactions.

Before setting up Apple Pay, let's briefly look at what it offers:

- **Apple Pay**: Apple Pay is Apple's digital payment system that allows you to add your credit, debit, and prepaid cards to your iPhone for seamless payments. Instead of using a physical card, you can use your iPhone's Face ID, Touch ID, or passcode to authenticate transactions at compatible payment terminals or online stores.
- **Wallet App**: The Wallet app on your iPhone 16 is where all your digital cards, tickets, and passes are stored. Besides storing credit and debit cards, you can add transit cards, event tickets, loyalty cards, boarding passes, and even student IDs, depending on the issuer's compatibility with Wallet. The Wallet app centralizes these items for quick access, making it a versatile digital companion.

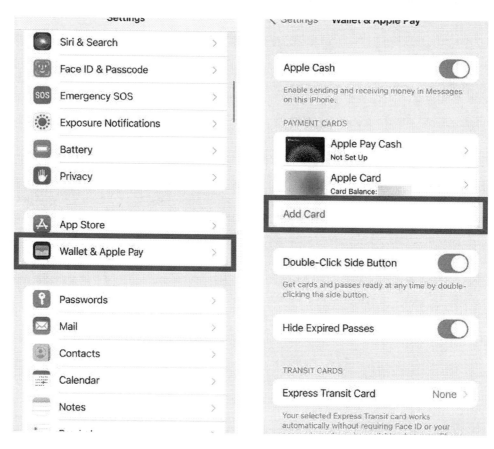

The setup process for Apple Pay involves adding a payment card to your Wallet, which enables you to make contactless payments. Here's how to get started:

- **Step 1: Open the Wallet App**:
  - » Open the Wallet app on your iPhone 16. If you haven't set up Apple Pay yet, you'll see a prompt to add a card.
- **Step 2: Add a Card**:
  - » Tap the **Add (+)** icon to begin adding a new card. You'll be prompted to choose the type of card you want to add, such as **Credit or Debit Card** or **Transit Card**.
  - » For this setup, select **Credit or Debit Card**.
- **Step 3: Scan or Enter Card Details**:
  - » You can either use your iPhone's camera to scan your card details or enter them manually. If you choose to scan, position the card within the frame, and your iPhone will automatically detect the card number and expiration date.
  - » If you prefer to enter the details manually, tap **Enter Card Details Manually** and type in the card number, expiration date, and security code.
- **Step 4: Verify Your Card**:
  - » After entering your card details, Apple Pay will prompt you to verify your card with your bank or card issuer. Verification methods vary by issuer but often include a text message or email code, a phone call, or an in-app prompt.

» Follow the instructions provided by your bank or card issuer to complete verification. Once verified, your card will be added to Wallet, and you'll be ready to start using Apple Pay.

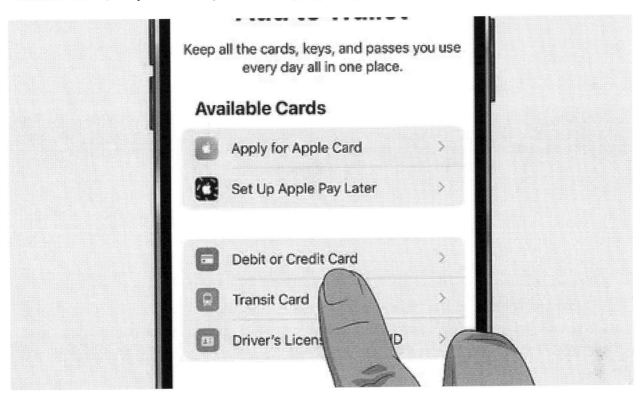

The Wallet app allows you to store a range of cards beyond just payment methods, making it a versatile tool for managing everyday essentials:

- **Adding Multiple Payment Cards**:
  » If you have more than one payment card, you can add multiple cards to your Wallet. Repeat the setup process for each card by tapping the **Add** button and following the same steps.
  » You can set a **default card** for Apple Pay transactions by going to **Settings > Wallet & Apple Pay** and selecting **Default Card** under **Transaction Defaults**.

- **Adding Loyalty and Rewards Cards**:
  » Many stores and services offer loyalty or rewards cards that can be added to Wallet. To add these, go to the Wallet app, tap **Add Card**, and select **Loyalty Card** or **Membership Card** if available.
  » Some apps, like those from airlines or retailers, allow you to add loyalty cards directly to Wallet by using their app, which then integrates with Wallet automatically.

- **Adding Transit Cards**:
  » In cities with compatible transit systems, you can add a transit card to Wallet and use your iPhone to tap into buses, trains, and subways. To add a transit card, select **Transit Card** when adding a new card, and follow the prompts for setup.
  » This feature is convenient for regular commuters, as it eliminates the need to carry a separate transit pass and can also allow for easy reloads within the Wallet app.

- **Adding Boarding Passes, Event Tickets, and More**:
  » If you have airline boarding passes, concert tickets, or event tickets, you can add them to Wallet by scanning a QR code or by tapping "Add to Apple Wallet" within an app or email confirmation.
  » Wallet will store these passes and present timely notifications for access when you arrive at the venue or airport, ensuring you have your tickets ready without needing to search for them.

If you use multiple Apple devices, you can add your cards to Apple Pay on each one to make payments easier:

- **Setting Up on Apple Watch**:

  » To set up Apple Pay on your Apple Watch, open the **Watch** app on your iPhone, tap **Wallet & Apple Pay**, and follow the steps to add a card. Each device has its own secure setup, so you'll need to add each card to each device manually.

- **Setting Up on iPad and Mac**:

  » You can also set up Apple Pay on compatible iPads and Macs for use in online purchases. Go to **Settings > Wallet & Apple Pay** on your iPad, or add Apple Pay to Safari on your Mac through **System Preferences**.

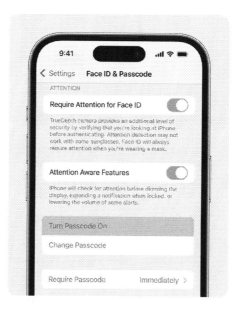

One of the main advantages of Apple Pay is the built-in security. Each transaction is authenticated with Face ID, Touch ID, or your passcode, making it secure and convenient:

- **Face ID or Touch ID**:

  » When you set up Apple Pay, Face ID or Touch ID will be enabled for payment verification, depending on your iPhone model. This adds an extra layer of security, as your device can only be unlocked by you, preventing unauthorized access.

- **Transaction-Specific Security**:

  » Apple Pay generates a unique transaction code each time you make a purchase, so your card number is never stored on your device or shared with the merchant. This approach reduces the risk of theft or fraud and ensures your card information remains private.

Once Apple Pay is set up, using it in stores, online, or within apps is quick and intuitive:

- **In-Store Payments**:
  - » To make a payment at a store, hold your iPhone near the contactless reader while pressing the side button to activate Face ID or Touch ID. Once authenticated, you'll see a checkmark on the screen indicating the payment was successful.

- **In-App and Online Purchases**:
  - » When shopping online or within apps, look for the **Apple Pay** button at checkout. Tap it to confirm your payment using Face ID, Touch ID, or your passcode. Apple Pay speeds up online transactions by eliminating the need to manually enter card information.

Over time, you may need to update your card details in Apple Pay, such as when a card expires or you receive a replacement card:

- **Updating Card Information**:
  - » If your card expires or changes, go to **Wallet**, tap on the card, and follow any prompts to update details. Your bank may also prompt you for re-verification if you receive a new card.

- **Removing Cards When Needed**:

» To remove a card, open **Wallet**, tap on the card, and select **Remove This Card**. This action removes it from Apple Pay but does not affect the physical card or its use elsewhere.

Setting up Apple Pay and the Wallet app on your iPhone 16 makes payments simpler and more secure. By adding your cards, organizing essential passes, and enabling Apple's security features, you can enjoy the convenience of a digital wallet that works seamlessly across devices. Whether you're paying for groceries, catching a train, or shopping online, Apple Pay and Wallet bring efficiency and security to every transaction, enhancing your iPhone's role as a reliable companion in daily life.

Making Payments Securely

With Apple Pay on your iPhone 16, making payments is not only convenient but also highly secure. Apple has built robust security features into Apple Pay to protect your personal and financial information, ensuring each transaction is private and secure. From advanced authentication methods like Face ID and Touch ID to unique transaction codes, Apple Pay reduces the risk of fraud and theft, making it a safer option than traditional cards or cash. In this section, we'll discuss the layers of security built into Apple Pay, how to make secure payments in stores, online, and within apps, and additional tips to keep your payment information safe.

Apple Pay's security is centered on several key features that work together to protect your information at every step of the payment process:

- **Device-Specific Card Numbers**:
  » When you add a credit or debit card to Apple Pay, Apple doesn't store the actual card number on your device. Instead, a unique **Device Account Number** is generated and stored securely in the device's **Secure Element**, a dedicated chip designed for secure data storage. Each Device Account Number is encrypted and tied only to that device, ensuring that your card details are never directly accessible on your iPhone.

- **Tokenization and Unique Transaction Codes**:
  » Each transaction made with Apple Pay uses a one-time unique transaction code, or "token," which ensures that your actual card information is never shared with the merchant. This means that if a data breach occurs at a store, the transaction information is useless to hackers because your card number is not stored or shared.

- **Authentication with Face ID, Touch ID, or Passcode**:
  » Apple Pay requires authentication with **Face ID**, **Touch ID**, or a device passcode for every transaction. This adds an extra layer of protection, as only you can authorize payments on your device. Even if someone else has access to your phone, they would be unable to complete a transaction without the required authentication.

Using Apple Pay in-store is a simple and safe process that requires minimal steps, thanks to contactless payment technology:

- **Step 1: Locate a Contactless Payment Terminal**:
  - » Look for the **contactless payment symbol** at the checkout. Most modern payment terminals in stores accept Apple Pay, making it easy to find compatible locations. Many stores also display an Apple Pay logo to indicate compatibility.

- **Step 2: Activate Apple Pay**:
  - » When you're ready to pay, double-click the side button on your iPhone if Face ID is enabled, or hold your finger on the **Touch ID** button if your iPhone model uses Touch ID. This action brings up Apple Pay and your default payment card.

- **Step 3: Hold Your Device Near the Reader**:
  - » Hold your iPhone near the contactless reader, usually located at the top or side of the payment terminal. Your iPhone will confirm payment with a small vibration and a checkmark on the screen, signaling that the transaction is complete.
  - » For additional security, Apple Pay verifies your payment with a unique one-time transaction code, keeping your card details private and unshared with the merchant.

- **Switching Cards for Payment**:
  - » If you want to use a different card, tap your default card in Apple Pay and select another from your Wallet before holding your iPhone near the reader. This flexibility makes it easy to choose the right payment method based on the purchase.

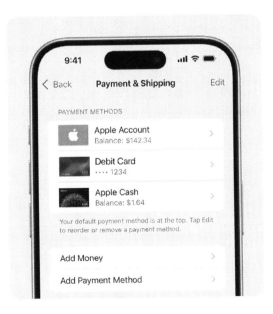

Apple Pay can also be used for purchases in apps and on websites, offering a secure, fast checkout experience without needing to manually enter payment information:

- **Identifying the Apple Pay Option**:
  - » When shopping online or in an app, look for the **Apple Pay** button at checkout. Many websites and apps include Apple Pay as a payment option, allowing you to complete transactions without entering your card number or billing information.
- **Confirming Your Payment**:
  - » After selecting Apple Pay at checkout, review your order details. Apple Pay will automatically fill in your shipping, billing, and payment information, streamlining the checkout process.
  - » Confirm your payment by using Face ID, Touch ID, or your device passcode. Once approved, you'll see a checkmark confirming that the transaction is complete.
- **Security Benefits for Online and In-App Payments**:
  - » Apple Pay reduces the risk of data theft by ensuring your card information isn't stored on third-party servers. Only your encrypted Device Account Number and unique transaction codes are used, offering additional privacy and security when shopping online.

Apple Pay is designed with privacy in mind, ensuring that your personal and payment information is kept private throughout the transaction process:

- **Minimal Data Collection**:
  - » Apple doesn't track or store information about your purchases. While Apple Pay keeps a limited record of recent transactions for your reference, it doesn't collect details about the items purchased or share this information with advertisers.
  - » Transaction data is only visible in your Wallet app for personal record-keeping, and it's limited to details like the merchant name, amount, and date. No additional information is stored or analyzed by Apple.
- **Bank-Level Security Standards**:
  - » Apple Pay meets or exceeds the security standards of financial institutions, using bank-grade encryption and security protocols to protect user information. Each bank or card issuer must authorize the use of Apple Pay, adding an extra layer of oversight and security.

While Apple Pay provides robust security features, you can take additional steps to ensure your information stays safe:

- **Use Face ID or Touch ID for Additional Security**:
    - » For optimal security, always use Face ID or Touch ID instead of your passcode when authenticating payments. Biometric authentication is harder to bypass, ensuring that only you can authorize purchases.

- **Monitor Your Transactions Regularly**:
    - » Regularly check your Wallet app or banking app for recent transactions to stay on top of your spending. Any unauthorized purchases or discrepancies should be reported to your bank or card issuer immediately for investigation.

- **Enable Find My iPhone**:
    - » If your iPhone is lost or stolen, **Find My iPhone** allows you to lock or erase the device remotely, preventing unauthorized access to Apple Pay and other sensitive information. Go to **Settings > [Your Name] > Find My** to make sure the feature is enabled.

- **Update Your iOS Software Regularly**:
    - » Apple regularly releases software updates that include security enhancements. Keeping your iPhone up to date ensures you benefit from the latest security protections available for Apple Pay and other features.

Apple Pay also includes **Apple Cash**, a convenient way to send and receive money from friends and family directly through the Messages app:

- **Setting Up Apple Cash**:
  - » To set up Apple Cash, go to **Settings > Wallet & Apple Pay** and follow the prompts to enable Apple Cash. Once set up, you can use it for peer-to-peer payments or even for in-store purchases.
- **Sending Money Securely**:
  - » In Messages, tap the **Apple Pay** icon, enter the amount, and confirm with Face ID or Touch ID. Apple Cash transactions are just as secure as Apple Pay purchases, using encrypted payment methods and unique transaction codes.
- **Using Apple Cash for Purchases**:
  - » You can use your Apple Cash balance for purchases within Apple Pay, providing flexibility and convenience. Your balance is stored securely within Wallet, and all transactions are protected by Apple Pay's security features.

With Apple Pay, you can manage multiple cards and even set a default card for your primary payments:

- **Setting a Default Card**:
  - » Go to **Settings > Wallet & Apple Pay** and select **Default Card** to choose which card Apple Pay will use by default. This feature is useful for setting up a primary card for everyday purchases, while still allowing easy switching to other cards when needed.
- **Switching Cards During Payment**:
  - » When making a purchase, simply tap your default card in Apple Pay to view your other cards. Selecting a different card is easy, allowing you to choose the best payment method for each situation.

Apple Pay works internationally, making it convenient for travelers. Here are some tips for using Apple Pay securely while abroad:

- **Checking with Your Bank**:
  - » Before traveling, check with your bank or card issuer to confirm that your card supports international Apple Pay transactions and to ensure there are no unexpected charges or restrictions.

- **Using Apple Pay for Currency Conversion**:
  - » Apple Pay handles currency conversion automatically, making it simple to pay in local currencies without additional hassle. Apple Pay charges your card in the local currency, just like a regular credit card transaction.

By using Apple Pay, you're choosing a payment method that prioritizes both convenience and security. Apple's combination of device-specific card numbers, transaction-specific security codes, and biometric authentication makes Apple Pay one of the most secure payment methods available today. From in-store purchases to online transactions, these protections ensure that your information stays private and that each transaction is securely verified. With a few additional security habits, like monitoring transactions and keeping your device updated, you can confidently rely on Apple Pay as a secure and streamlined way to handle all your payments.

Tips for Managing Payment Information

With the growing adoption of digital wallets like Apple Pay, managing payment information on your iPhone has never been easier. Properly organizing and managing your payment details within Apple Pay and the Wallet app can enhance security, streamline purchases, and provide peace of mind. From keeping track of multiple cards to securing your information, this section offers valuable tips for effectively managing your payment information on your iPhone 16.

The Wallet app can hold multiple cards, including credit, debit, and even loyalty or gift cards. Organizing these helps you make quick, easy payments and manage finances efficiently:

- **Add All Relevant Cards to Wallet**:
  » Add all frequently used credit, debit, and store cards to your Wallet app for seamless access. To do this, open the Wallet app, tap the **Add (+)** icon, and follow the prompts to add a new card by scanning it or entering details manually.

- **Set a Default Payment Card**:
  » Setting a default card allows for a quicker checkout process. To do so, go to **Settings > Wallet & Apple Pay**, scroll to **Transaction Defaults**, and select **Default Card**. Your default card will automatically be used unless you select another at the time of purchase.

- **Label Cards for Easy Recognition**:
  » If you have multiple cards in Wallet, give them clear nicknames to help differentiate between them. You can label cards based on their type or use, such as "Groceries" or "Travel," helping you choose the right card in an instant.

Keeping an eye on your transactions is essential for effective management and fraud prevention. Apple Pay offers features to review your recent transactions directly in Wallet:

- **Check Recent Purchases in Wallet**:

» Open Wallet and tap on any card to view recent transactions. Apple Pay displays the merchant name, location, and amount, allowing you to monitor your spending patterns and verify charges.

- **Set Up Alerts for Spending and Purchases**:

  » Some banks offer alert services for purchases or unusual activity, which can be enabled in the bank's app or website. These alerts provide real-time notifications on spending, helping you quickly detect unauthorized transactions or overspending.

- **Regularly Compare Statements**:

  » For thorough record-keeping, compare Apple Pay's transaction history with your monthly bank or credit card statements. This extra check ensures that all purchases are correct and helps you stay on top of your financial habits.

Ensuring the security of your payment information is crucial. Apple Pay is inherently secure, but additional precautions can further protect your payment data:

- **Enable Face ID, Touch ID, or Passcode Protection**:

  » Always use **Face ID**, **Touch ID**, or a secure passcode to protect your Wallet. These authentication methods ensure that only you can access Apple Pay, preventing unauthorized purchases if your device is lost or stolen.

- **Use Two-Factor Authentication (2FA)**:

  » Enable two-factor authentication on your Apple ID for added security. 2FA ensures that your Wallet can only be accessed by you, even if someone else gains access to your Apple ID credentials. Set this up by going to **Settings > [Your Name] > Password & Security > Two-Factor Authentication**.

- **Regularly Update Your iOS Software**:

  » Keeping your iPhone up to date with the latest iOS version provides you with Apple's newest security features and bug fixes. Updates can help patch vulnerabilities, reducing the risk of data breaches or unauthorized access.

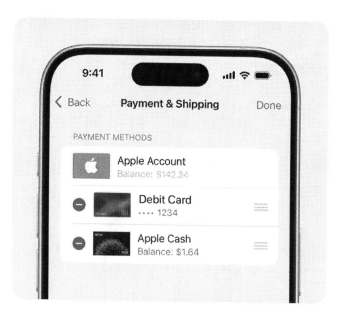

Keeping your payment information current is essential for seamless transactions and avoiding declined purchases due to expired cards:

- **Update Expired Cards Promptly**:
  - » When you receive a new card to replace an expired one, remember to update it in Apple Pay. To do so, open Wallet, select the expired card, and tap **Remove This Card**. Then add the new card by following the usual setup steps.

- **Removing Unused or Inactive Cards**:
  - » Removing old, unused, or inactive cards from Wallet helps keep your payment methods organized and reduces clutter. To remove a card, go to Wallet, tap on the card, and select **Remove This Card**. This action also helps reduce confusion when selecting cards at checkout.

- **Monitor Credit Card Limit Notifications**:
  - » Some banks offer notifications when you're approaching your credit limit. Monitoring these alerts helps you stay aware of your credit usage and manage your finances more effectively, avoiding accidental overages or interest charges.

Apple Pay can simplify recurring payments for subscriptions or bills, making it easier to manage regular expenses:

- **Setting Up Apple Pay for Subscriptions**:

» Many subscription services, including streaming platforms and app subscriptions, support Apple Pay. By selecting Apple Pay as your payment method for these services, you can easily manage and review all subscriptions in one place.

- **Using Apple Pay for Monthly Bills**:

  » Some utility companies, phone providers, and insurance companies accept Apple Pay for monthly payments. Check with your service providers to see if this is an option, as it can streamline your bill management and ensure timely payments.

- **Reviewing Subscription Charges in Wallet**:

  » By using Apple Pay for subscriptions, you can view and verify all recurring charges directly in Wallet. This helps you track your monthly spending on services and make adjustments if necessary, such as canceling unused subscriptions.

Apple Cash is a convenient, secure way to send money to friends and family or to use for small purchases. Here's how to manage it effectively:

- **Set Up and Enable Apple Cash**:

  » To start using Apple Cash, go to **Settings > Wallet & Apple Pay** and follow the setup prompts. Once enabled, you can send and receive money through the Messages app.

- **Monitor Apple Cash Balance and Transactions**:

  » Apple Cash maintains a transaction history, which you can view in Wallet. This helps you track all funds sent, received, and spent, ensuring you always know your balance and transaction history.

- **Transfer Apple Cash to Your Bank**:

  » If you prefer to keep a low balance in Apple Cash, transfer funds to your bank account by going to **Wallet > Apple Cash > Transfer to Bank**. This option helps you manage your cash flow and keeps your main accounts consolidated.

Privacy is a core feature of Apple Pay, but taking a few extra steps can enhance your personal data protection:

- **Limit Data Sharing with Merchants**:
  - » Apple Pay doesn't share your card number with merchants, reducing data exposure. For additional privacy, you can avoid linking loyalty or rewards programs directly to Apple Pay, unless absolutely necessary, which minimizes data collection from third parties.

- **Review Privacy Settings in Wallet**:
  - » Apple Pay includes settings to manage how data is shared with merchants. Go to **Settings > Privacy > Wallet & Apple Pay** to adjust permissions and ensure you're comfortable with the level of data shared during transactions.

- **Review Permissions for Location-Based Notifications**:
  - » Wallet can send location-based notifications for nearby merchants or rewards, but if you prefer not to receive these, go to **Settings > Privacy > Location Services > Wallet** to adjust or disable location-based notifications.

Apple Pay can be used internationally, but preparing for travel ensures smooth transactions:

- **Check with Your Bank for International Compatibility**:
  - » Not all banks and cards are compatible with Apple Pay abroad. Contact your bank to confirm if your card will work internationally with Apple Pay and inquire about any fees for foreign transactions.

- **Enable International Transaction Alerts**:
  - » If your bank offers international alerts, enabling them helps you stay informed of foreign purchases and detect any suspicious activity while traveling. Alerts can help you manage exchange rates and monitor spending in different currencies.

- **Monitor Exchange Rates and Currency Settings**:
  - » Apple Pay handles currency conversion automatically, but keeping an eye on exchange rates can help you understand your spending while abroad. Some banking apps offer live exchange rates for easier management of international transactions.

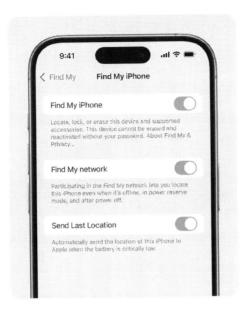

In case of lost or stolen devices, knowing how to secure your payment information is essential:

- **Enable Find My iPhone for Remote Locking**:
  - » **Find My iPhone** allows you to lock or erase your device remotely, protecting your Wallet information if your iPhone is lost or stolen. Go to **Settings > [Your Name] > Find My** to ensure the feature is enabled.

- **Prepare Alternative Payment Methods**:
  - » While Apple Pay is highly convenient, keeping an alternative payment method, such as a physical card, available can prevent inconveniences if your iPhone is lost or out of battery.

- **Know How to Suspend Apple Pay**:
  - » If your iPhone is lost, you can quickly suspend Apple Pay by marking your device as lost in the **Find My iPhone** app or by contacting your bank. Suspending Apple Pay secures your account information until you locate your device or get a replacement.

Effectively managing your payment information in Apple Pay and Wallet on your iPhone 16 offers convenience, security, and control over your finances. By organizing cards, reviewing transactions, securing your account, and taking precautions for privacy, you can enjoy the benefits of digital payments with confidence. Whether you're using Apple Pay for in-store purchases, managing subscriptions, or sending money to friends, these practices ensure a smooth, secure, and efficient experience. With a few mindful habits, your digital wallet will be a reliable and organized tool for handling everyday financial interactions.

CHAPTER 11
HEALTH & FITNESS

Welcome to Chapter 11: Health & Fitness! The iPhone 16 offers a powerful suite of tools to help you stay active, track your wellness, and manage your health—all through the Health app. With features designed to monitor your physical activity, manage medical information, and support mindfulness and sleep, the Health app turns your iPhone into a personal health companion that supports you every day. In this chapter, we'll explore how to use these tools to create a routine that enhances your physical, mental, and emotional well-being.

We'll start by looking at **Using the Health App for Activity Tracking**. Tracking your activity with the Health app is easy and effective. The app collects data on your steps, distance walked, and other physical activities, giving you a clear picture of your daily movement. With customizable goals and trends, you'll be able to set activity targets that align with your fitness level and track your progress over time. For those with an Apple Watch, this data syncs seamlessly, adding even more detail to your health insights.

Next, we'll guide you through **Setting Up Medical ID and Emergency Contacts**. The Medical ID feature stores important health information that can be accessed in case of emergency, such as allergies, medical conditions, and emergency contact information. Having this information readily available could be life-saving, as first responders can access it from the Lock Screen without unlocking your phone. We'll walk you through the setup, so your critical health details are always available if needed.

Finally, we'll explore **Mindfulness and Sleep Tracking**. With tools to help you manage stress, meditate, and track sleep patterns, the Health app supports mental well-being as well as physical health. Whether you're trying to create a calming bedtime routine, meditate to reduce stress, or understand your sleep cycles better, the Health app has features that can help. Mindfulness and sleep tracking are valuable components of a balanced health routine, and incorporating these practices into your day-to-day life can improve both your energy levels and peace of mind.

By the end of this chapter, you'll feel confident in using your iPhone to manage various aspects of your health, from daily physical activity to emergency preparedness and mental wellness. The Health app's user-friendly interface and diverse tools empower you to take control of your health, building routines that enhance your quality of life. Let's dive into each feature and explore how to make your iPhone a powerful partner in supporting your health and fitness journey.

Using the Health App for Activity Tracking

The Health app on your iPhone 16 is a powerful tool for tracking daily physical activities, providing insights into your overall health, and helping you set and achieve fitness goals. Whether you're interested in monitoring your daily steps, tracking your workouts, or keeping an eye on key health metrics, the Health app collects and organizes this data in one easy-to-access location. In this section, we'll walk you through using the Health app for activity tracking, including setting goals, understanding data, and syncing with other devices for enhanced insights.

The Health app on your iPhone 16 is designed to be intuitive and user-friendly, allowing you to start tracking activities with ease:

- **Opening the Health App**:

  » Locate the **Health** app on your Home Screen, marked by a white icon with a red heart. Open the app to access your health dashboard, where you'll see various categories, including Activity, Heart, Mindfulness, and more.

  » Upon opening, you may be prompted to enter some basic information, such as your age, height, and weight. This data helps the app provide more accurate health metrics, especially for calorie estimates and step count calculations.

- **Setting Up the Health App**:

  » On your initial setup, you'll see the **Summary** tab, which displays key health information like steps, distance walked, and flights climbed. You can customize this view to display the health metrics most important to you by selecting **Edit** at the bottom of the screen.

  » Choose the metrics you want to track, such as Active Energy, Steps, and Walking Distance. The Summary tab will provide a quick glance at your daily progress in these areas, motivating you to stay active throughout the day.

The Health app uses your iPhone's built-in sensors to track basic physical activity data, including steps, distance walked, and flights climbed. Here's how each metric works and how to use this information to stay active:

- **Steps**:

- » The Health app counts your steps automatically throughout the day. Steps are recorded in the background, so you don't need to open the app to start tracking. To view your daily step count, go to **Summary > Steps**.
- » Steps are an easy way to gauge your daily activity. The Health app displays a daily step goal and shows your progress, which you can adjust to match your fitness level. For instance, you can aim for the widely recommended 10,000 steps a day or set a personalized goal.

- **Walking and Running Distance**:
  - » Besides steps, the Health app tracks the total distance you've covered while walking or running. This metric is especially useful for users who prefer distance-based goals, like walking a mile every morning.
  - » To see your walking or running distance, navigate to **Summary > Walking + Running Distance**. The app provides daily, weekly, and monthly distance summaries, so you can monitor trends and set specific distance goals over time.

- **Flights Climbed**:
  - » Using the iPhone's barometric sensor, the Health app also tracks the number of flights you climb. This can be a helpful measure if you're focused on leg strength or cardiovascular health, as climbing stairs is a great way to elevate your heart rate.
  - » View flights climbed under **Summary > Flights Climbed**. Tracking this metric encourages small lifestyle changes, like choosing stairs over elevators, to incorporate more movement into your day.

Setting goals in the Health app helps you stay motivated and focused on your fitness journey. Here's how to set and customize daily activity goals:

- **Customizing Step Goals**:
  - » While the Health app doesn't have a built-in feature for custom step goals, you can set reminders or use the **Activity** section to motivate yourself to reach a certain number of steps each day. For example, you can set a daily reminder to check your progress halfway through the day.
  - » Alternatively, you can set reminders on your Apple Watch (if you have one) to prompt you to stand up, move, and reach your target step count.

- **Tracking Active Energy**:
  - » Active Energy, also known as calories burned, is a helpful metric for users interested in weight management or caloric balance. To view Active Energy, go to **Summary > Active Energy**. This section displays estimated calories burned from physical activities throughout the day.
  - » You can set daily or weekly Active Energy goals by adjusting your preferred calorie target. Monitoring this goal can help you stay active and maintain a balance between calorie intake and expenditure.

- **Using Streaks and Trends for Motivation**:

» One of the most powerful features of the Health app is its ability to display streaks and activity trends over time. For instance, the app shows your weekly averages for steps, distance, and Active Energy.

» Seeing consistent improvements or identifying areas where activity has decreased can be motivating. Aim to build streaks by hitting your targets regularly, and use the Trends section to understand and adjust your activity levels over time.

While the iPhone's sensors can track basic metrics, using an Apple Watch or third-party apps enhances your Health app data by adding more details and specificity:

• **Syncing with Apple Watch**:

» If you have an Apple Watch, it automatically syncs with your Health app, providing even more accurate activity data, such as calories burned, heart rate, and specific workout types (e.g., running, cycling, or swimming).

» The Apple Watch's **Activity Rings** feature tracks **Move, Exercise, and Stand** goals, offering a visual representation of your daily activity. Closing these rings daily or weekly can be an engaging way to stay active and motivated.

• **Connecting Third-Party Apps**:

» The Health app supports data from various fitness apps, such as MyFitnessPal, Strava, or Nike Run Club. To connect a third-party app, go to **Settings > Health > Data Access & Devices**, select the app, and enable sharing of relevant health data.

» Third-party apps can provide specific data like nutrition tracking, workout details, or specialized health metrics (e.g., running pace), enriching your overall health profile within the Health app.

Tracking your activity trends over time allows you to understand your habits and make adjustments for better health. Here's how to review historical data and interpret trends:

- **Accessing Weekly and Monthly Summaries**:
  - » The Health app allows you to view data summaries by day, week, month, or year, which provides a comprehensive overview of your activity levels over time. Tap on any metric (e.g., Steps or Active Energy) and select **Show All Data** to view historical information.
  - » Weekly and monthly summaries can reveal patterns, helping you see if you're meeting your activity goals consistently. This information can also help identify when you might be less active, such as weekends, allowing you to make lifestyle adjustments.

- **Analyzing Trends and Patterns**:
  - » In the **Trends** section, the Health app shows whether you're trending up or down in various categories, such as steps, distance, and energy. Positive trends indicate that you're increasing activity, while negative trends suggest a decrease.
  - » Use these trends to set new goals, challenge yourself to improve, and keep track of your long-term health journey. For example, if your steps are trending down, aim to increase activity by adding a daily walk.

The Health app doesn't just track activity—it provides insights based on your data, making it easier to make informed health decisions:

- **Receiving Health Recommendations**:
  - » Apple's Health app occasionally provides personalized health tips or reminders based on your activity data. For instance, if your exercise level drops, you may receive a suggestion to increase daily movement.
  - » These recommendations can serve as reminders to stay active or offer tips to improve specific aspects of your fitness routine.
- **Sharing Health Data with Medical Professionals**:
  - » You can share specific Health app data with healthcare providers if they support Health app integration. This feature is beneficial if you want to discuss your activity trends with a doctor or a personal trainer, as it gives them a clearer picture of your lifestyle habits.
- **Using Health Sharing with Family**:
  - » For added motivation or support, use **Health Sharing** to share selected health data with family members. This feature can help family members stay accountable to their activity goals and support each other in maintaining healthy habits.

The Health app's activity tracking features on your iPhone 16 are designed to help you lead an active, healthy lifestyle. By setting goals, monitoring your daily steps, tracking Active Energy, and analyzing trends, you'll be able to make informed decisions about your health and adjust your habits to meet your goals. Whether you're just beginning to track your activity or looking to build on existing fitness routines, the Health app offers powerful tools that simplify and support your wellness journey.

Setting Up Medical ID and Emergency Contacts

Setting up Medical ID and emergency contacts on your iPhone 16 is one of the most important steps you can take to prepare for unexpected health situations. Medical ID allows you to store essential health information—like allergies, medical conditions, medications, and emergency contacts—that can be accessed directly from the Lock Screen by first responders. This information can be life-saving, especially if you're unable to communicate in an emergency. In this section, we'll guide you through setting up your Medical ID and emergency contacts, ensuring that crucial health details are always accessible if needed.

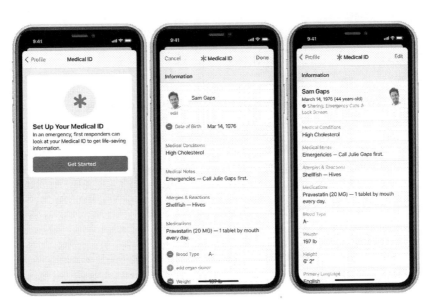

Medical ID is designed to provide critical health information in an emergency, potentially assisting first responders in making quick, informed decisions about your care:

- **Key Information at a Glance**:
  - » Medical ID allows you to store your name, date of birth, medical conditions, allergies, medications, blood type, and

other essential health details. First responders can access this information quickly to understand your medical history and avoid administering medications that may interact with your current prescriptions or conditions.

- **Access from the Lock Screen**:

  » Medical ID is accessible even when your iPhone is locked. By swiping up on the Lock Screen, anyone can tap **Emergency** and then **Medical ID** to view your health information and emergency contacts. This feature ensures that vital information is available to healthcare professionals or family members, regardless of access to your phone's passcode.

Setting up Medical ID is straightforward and takes only a few minutes. Here's a step-by-step guide to entering your health details:

- **Step 1: Open the Health App**:

  » Open the **Health** app from your Home Screen. If this is your first time using the app, you may be prompted to set up some basic health information. Tap on the **Browse** tab and then tap **Medical ID**.

- **Step 2: Start Creating Your Medical ID**:

  » Tap **Get Started** or **Edit** if you've previously entered any information. This will bring up a form where you can input essential health data.

- **Step 3: Enter Personal Information**:

  » The Medical ID form allows you to add your **name, date of birth**, and **photo**. Including this information helps first responders confirm your identity and refer to your health details quickly.

- **Step 4: Input Medical Conditions and Allergies**:

  » Scroll down to the **Medical Conditions** and **Allergies & Reactions** sections. Add any relevant health conditions, such as diabetes, hypertension, or asthma, along with allergies to medications or foods. Accurate information here can help avoid harmful treatments and ensure safe care.

- **Step 5: List Medications and Blood Type**:

  » In the **Medications** section, list any medications you're currently taking, especially if they're essential for ongoing health management (e.g., heart medications or blood thinners). You can also add your **Blood Type**, which can be critical information if a blood transfusion is needed.

- **Step 6: Add Organ Donor Status**:

  » There is an **Organ Donor** option in the Medical ID setup. If you're registered as an organ donor, indicate this status. Knowing this can inform medical decisions if you're involved in a severe accident or health crisis.

Emergency contacts are a vital component of Medical ID. When added, these contacts can be notified if Emergency SOS is activated. Here's how to add them:

- **Step 1: Locate Emergency Contact Section**:
  » In the Medical ID form, scroll to the **Emergency Contacts** section and tap **Add Emergency Contact**. This action will open your contacts list.

- **Step 2: Select Contacts from Your Address Book**:
  » Choose a contact from your phone's address book. You'll be prompted to specify their relationship to you, such as spouse, sibling, or friend. Repeat this process to add multiple contacts if desired.

- **Step 3: Verify Contact Information**:
  » Ensure that the phone numbers for your emergency contacts are accurate and up to date. Emergency contacts will receive notifications when you activate Emergency SOS, so make sure you select individuals who can respond promptly.

- **Step 4: Saving and Enabling Access from Lock Screen**:
  » After entering all details, scroll to the top and toggle on **Show When Locked**. This setting allows Medical ID to be accessible from the Lock Screen without needing your passcode, making it easy for first responders to access the information in emergencies.
  » Tap **Done** to save your Medical ID. You can return to the Health app anytime to edit or update your information.

The Emergency SOS feature on your iPhone 16 automatically contacts emergency services and notifies your emergency contacts. Here's how to activate and customize it:

- **Step 1: Enable Emergency SOS**:

  » Go to **Settings > Emergency SOS**. Here, you'll see two options: **Call with Hold** and **Call with 5 Presses**.

  » **Call with Hold** lets you press and hold the side button and one of the volume buttons simultaneously to activate SOS, while **Call with 5 Presses** allows you to press the side button five times quickly. Both methods will initiate an emergency call and alert your contacts.

- **Step 2: Customize Emergency Contacts Notification**:

  » When you activate Emergency SOS, your emergency contacts will receive a text message with your location, even if Location Services is disabled. This message also updates if your location changes within a certain timeframe, helping your contacts track your whereabouts.

- **Step 3: Practicing Activation**:

  » Familiarize yourself with activating Emergency SOS so you're comfortable using it in a real emergency. Be cautious not to hold the buttons too long during practice, as you might inadvertently call emergency services.

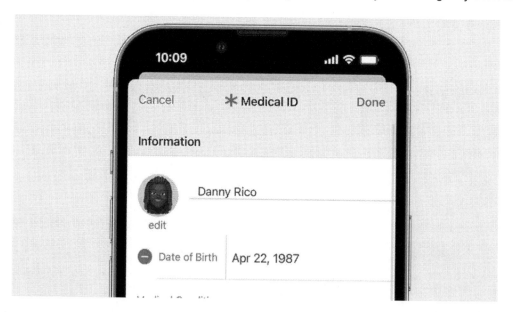

Keeping your Medical ID up to date is essential, as your health information and emergency contacts may change over time:

- **Review Health Details Periodically**:
  - » Update your Medical ID if there are any changes in your medical conditions, medications, or allergies. This ensures that first responders and healthcare providers always have the most current information, which could be crucial in an emergency.
- **Updating Contact Information**:
  - » Review and update emergency contact information if your contacts change phone numbers, or if you want to assign someone else as an emergency contact. Open the Health app, go to **Medical ID**, and tap **Edit** to make changes as needed.
- **Consider Changes in Health Status**:
  - » If your health status changes significantly, such as following a new diagnosis or treatment, update your Medical ID to reflect these changes. For example, adding information about a new medication or an allergy can be critical.

Sharing information about your Medical ID with family members or close friends ensures they understand how to access your health information in an emergency:

- **Show Family Members How to Access Medical ID**:
  - » Demonstrate to family members how to access Medical ID from your iPhone's Lock Screen. This can be done by swiping up, tapping **Emergency**, and selecting **Medical ID**. Sharing this information can help family or friends assist emergency responders if you're unable to communicate.
- **Encourage Family to Set Up Their Medical IDs**:
  - » Encourage family members to set up their own Medical IDs, especially if they have health conditions or take medications. This preparation can be helpful for family safety, as everyone will have their emergency information readily available.

7. Using Health Sharing for Emergency Preparedness

Apple's Health app offers a **Health Sharing** feature, allowing you to share select health data with family members or healthcare providers:

- **Setting Up Health Sharing**:
  - » Go to **Health > Sharing**, select **Share with Someone**, and choose a contact from your list. You can customize which health metrics to share, such as activity levels, heart rate, or other relevant health data.
  - » Health Sharing keeps family or caregivers informed about your health trends, adding an extra layer of safety in case of emergencies.

- **Customizing Shared Data**:
  - » If you prefer not to share certain information, select only the categories that are relevant. Health Sharing is customizable, allowing you to maintain privacy while still keeping loved ones informed about important health metrics.

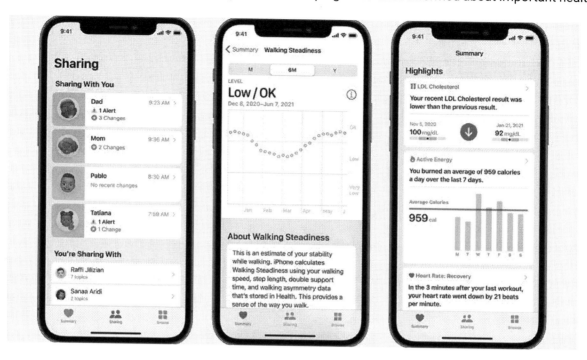

Testing access to your Medical ID and practicing Emergency SOS activation gives you confidence that these tools are ready if you need them:

- **Testing Medical ID Access**:
  - » To verify that your Medical ID is accessible, lock your phone, swipe up to access the Lock Screen, and tap **Emergency**. Then, select **Medical ID** to see if your health details and emergency contacts appear. Testing ensures that the feature is set up properly.

- **Practicing Emergency SOS Activation**:
  - » Practice activating Emergency SOS by gently pressing the buttons without holding long enough to call emergency services. Knowing how to activate it quickly can make a big difference in an emergency, so practice until you're comfortable with the procedure.

Setting up Medical ID and emergency contacts on your iPhone 16 is a proactive step toward ensuring your safety in emergency situations. By entering key health information, designating emergency contacts, and activating Emergency SOS, you make essential details accessible to first responders and loved ones when it matters most. Taking time to set up and maintain this information provides peace of mind, knowing that your health data is readily available, offering you and your family an added layer of security and preparedness.

Exploring Mindfulness and Sleep Tracking

The iPhone 16 offers powerful tools to help you improve mental wellness and understand your sleep patterns, all accessible through the Health app. With built-in mindfulness and sleep-tracking features, your iPhone can guide you in developing routines that support both mental and physical well-being. Mindfulness exercises can help you manage stress, build focus, and feel more centered, while sleep tracking allows you to understand your sleep quality and set up habits that lead to better rest. In this section, we'll explore how to use these features to support relaxation, enhance mindfulness, and improve sleep quality, creating a balanced approach to health.

Mindfulness is the practice of staying present and aware of your thoughts, feelings, and surroundings. Practicing mindfulness has been shown to reduce stress, improve focus, and enhance emotional resilience, making it an essential tool for modern life. The iPhone's Health app, along with various third-party apps, offers easy ways to incorporate mindfulness practices into your daily routine:

- **Reduced Stress and Anxiety**:
  - » Regular mindfulness exercises can help reduce stress by teaching you to stay focused on the present moment, allowing you to manage stressful situations calmly and avoid overthinking or worrying about future events.

- **Improved Focus and Productivity**:
  - » Practicing mindfulness also improves focus and concentration by training your mind to return to the present whenever it wanders. This can be especially helpful in daily tasks, work, or study environments.

- **Better Emotional Awareness and Balance**:
  - » Mindfulness increases awareness of your emotions, helping you to manage them without reacting impulsively. This greater emotional balance supports positive relationships and can make daily interactions more fulfilling.

The Health app on your iPhone 16 allows you to track your mindfulness activities, providing a record of your sessions and helping you establish consistency in your practice:

- **Setting Up Mindfulness Tracking**:
  - » Open the **Health** app, tap **Browse** at the bottom, and select **Mindfulness** from the categories. Here, you can track the time you spend on mindfulness exercises. If you use the **Breathe** app on Apple Watch or any mindfulness apps that sync with Health, those sessions will appear here automatically.
  - » You can also set a daily goal for mindfulness minutes, helping you build a consistent routine. Tracking minutes encourages you to dedicate time daily or weekly to mindfulness, improving your mental well-being over time.
- **Adding Mindfulness Sessions Manually**:
  - » If you practice mindfulness without an app or device, you can still log these sessions manually in the Health app. Tap **Add Data** in the Mindfulness section, enter the duration and time of the session, and save it. This way, you can keep a record of all your practices, even those done without digital assistance.

Several apps available on the App Store offer guided mindfulness exercises that sync with your Health app, making it easier to track your progress and stay committed to the practice:

- **Apple's Breathe App (Apple Watch)**:
  - » If you have an Apple Watch, the **Breathe** app is a convenient way to incorporate short breathing exercises into your day. These exercises last a few minutes and guide you to focus on your breath, helping you reduce stress and center yourself.
  - » The Breathe app syncs automatically with the Health app, so you can see your mindfulness minutes add up. The watch also reminds you to take breathing breaks, gently encouraging you to make mindfulness a habit.
- **Calm and Headspace (Third-Party Apps)**:
  - » **Calm** and **Headspace** are two popular mindfulness apps that offer a wide range of guided sessions, including meditation, deep breathing, and sleep stories. These apps help beginners and experienced practitioners alike, with sessions that focus on relaxation, anxiety reduction, and mental clarity.
  - » Both apps integrate with the Health app, allowing you to track your sessions and maintain consistency in your mindfulness routine. They also offer reminders, progress trackers, and themed programs, making it easier to stay committed to your practice.

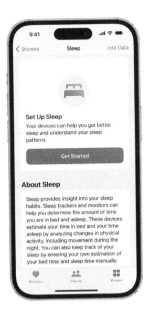

Sleep is essential for physical health, mental clarity, and emotional resilience. The Health app's sleep-tracking feature helps you understand your sleep patterns and create a bedtime routine that improves your rest:

- **Accessing Sleep Settings**:
  - » Go to the Health app, tap **Browse**, and select **Sleep**. You'll find options for setting up sleep tracking, viewing sleep data, and adjusting your bedtime schedule.

- **Setting a Sleep Schedule**:
  - » Tap **Full Schedule & Options** to set up a regular bedtime and wake-up time. Creating a consistent sleep schedule can help regulate your body's internal clock, leading to more restful sleep.
  - » You can customize your sleep schedule by adjusting your desired sleep duration, setting different schedules for weekdays and weekends, and adding reminders to help you wind down before bed.

- **Using Bedtime Reminders and Wind Down Mode**:
  - » Wind Down is a feature that helps you transition smoothly to bedtime by setting a specific time before bed for calming activities, like reading or meditating. During Wind Down, your iPhone's notifications will dim, and a simplified screen will appear to minimize distractions.
  - » To set up Wind Down, go to **Sleep > Full Schedule & Options > Wind Down** and choose how long before bed you'd like to activate it. This quiet time prepares your mind and body for sleep, signaling that it's time to relax.

If you want more detailed insights into your sleep, pairing your iPhone with an Apple Watch or sleep-tracking apps can provide additional data:

- **Sleep Tracking with Apple Watch**:
  - » If you have an Apple Watch, it can track your sleep duration and quality, syncing this data to the Health app automatically. Apple Watch monitors your heart rate and motion throughout the night, providing a clearer picture of your rest.
  - » With Apple Watch, you can also track how long you spend in each sleep stage (e.g., light, deep, REM sleep), which can help you understand your sleep cycles and make adjustments for better rest.

- **Sleep Cycle and AutoSleep (Third-Party Apps)**:
  - » **Sleep Cycle** and **AutoSleep** are popular third-party sleep-tracking apps that provide in-depth insights into your sleep patterns. These apps can track sleep quality, detect snoring, and even use smart alarms to wake you during a lighter sleep phase for a more refreshed start to your day.
  - » Both apps sync with the Health app, enabling you to review detailed sleep data alongside your other health metrics. They also offer tips on improving sleep quality based on your data trends.

Tracking your mindfulness and sleep data over time allows you to see patterns, adjust routines, and set achievable goals for both mental and physical well-being:

- **Viewing Trends Over Time**:
  - » In the Health app, you can view weekly and monthly summaries for both mindfulness and sleep data. These summaries reveal trends, helping you see if you're maintaining consistent habits or need to make adjustments.
  - » Recognizing trends, like improved focus from mindfulness or more consistent sleep durations, can reinforce positive behaviors and motivate you to stay committed.

- **Identifying Areas for Improvement**:
  - » Reviewing your data can help you pinpoint areas to improve. For example, if you notice poor sleep quality or less time in deep sleep, try adjusting your bedtime routine or implementing Wind Down activities.
  - » If your mindfulness practice is inconsistent, set reminders or consider shorter sessions to make it easier to incorporate mindfulness into your day.

Using the Health app, you can set goals for mindfulness minutes and sleep duration, helping you stay on track and encouraging gradual improvement:

- **Daily or Weekly Mindfulness Goals**:
  - » Decide on a realistic daily or weekly goal for mindfulness, like 10–15 minutes per day, and use reminders or app notifications to help you meet this target. Starting with small, achievable goals makes it easier to build a habit.

- **Targeting Ideal Sleep Duration**:
  - » The Health app lets you set a goal for sleep duration, typically between 7–9 hours per night. Adjust this goal based on your needs, and experiment with routines that help you reach it. Tracking your progress motivates you to prioritize sleep, reinforcing its importance in your daily routine.

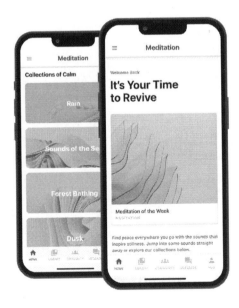

Consistency is key to reaping the benefits of mindfulness and quality sleep. Here are some tips to integrate these practices into your everyday life:

- **Mindfulness Reminders Throughout the Day**:
  - » Schedule mindfulness breaks during your day, even if it's just 5 minutes to breathe deeply or focus on gratitude. Regular mindfulness breaks improve your overall mental well-being, keeping stress levels low and enhancing focus.

- **Developing a Relaxing Bedtime Routine**:

» A calming bedtime routine is essential for better sleep. Try incorporating light stretching, deep breathing exercises, or reading to ease into restfulness. These habits signal to your body that it's time to wind down, supporting your sleep goals.

Using your iPhone 16's Health app for mindfulness and sleep tracking gives you valuable insights into your mental and physical wellness. By setting goals, tracking your progress, and implementing routines, you can cultivate practices that improve focus, reduce stress, and enhance sleep quality. These tools empower you to take charge of your well-being, making mindfulness and restful sleep an integral part of a balanced and healthy lifestyle.

CHAPTER 12
TROUBLESHOOTING AND MAINTENANCE

Welcome to Chapter 12: Troubleshooting and Maintenance! As with any device, occasional issues may arise with your iPhone 16, but knowing how to troubleshoot and perform regular maintenance can keep it running smoothly and extend its lifespan. From fixing common connection problems to managing battery life and backing up data, this chapter covers essential tips and tools to ensure your iPhone remains reliable and efficient.

We'll begin with **Common Fixes for Wi-Fi, Bluetooth, and Apps**. It's not unusual for Wi-Fi or Bluetooth connections to occasionally drop, or for apps to freeze or crash. These are typical issues for any smartphone, and they're usually easy to resolve. In this section, we'll cover step-by-step instructions on diagnosing and fixing these common problems. Whether it's reconnecting to a Wi-Fi network, troubleshooting Bluetooth connections, or getting an unresponsive app back up and running, you'll gain confidence in quickly resolving minor glitches.

Next, we'll discuss **Managing Battery Life and Storage**. Battery life and storage space are essential factors in maintaining a smooth, fast iPhone experience. Over time, certain settings, background activities, and apps can drain your battery or fill up storage, impacting the phone's performance. We'll go over settings adjustments, app management tips, and storage-clearing strategies to maximize battery efficiency and keep your device clutter-free. By taking proactive steps, you can avoid running out of power at inconvenient times and ensure you have enough space for new photos, apps, and updates.

Finally, we'll explore **Backing Up and Restoring Data with iCloud**. Backing up your iPhone is crucial for protecting your data in case of loss, damage, or upgrade. With iCloud, backing up is a seamless process that saves your settings, app data, photos, and more, making it easy to restore everything to a new device if needed. This section will guide you through setting up automatic iCloud backups, managing backup storage, and restoring your data from an iCloud backup. We'll also touch on using iCloud for device syncing, keeping your information updated across all your Apple devices.

By the end of this chapter, you'll be equipped with the knowledge and skills to troubleshoot common issues, optimize battery life and storage, and secure your data through regular backups. These maintenance tips will help you get the most out of your iPhone 16, ensuring it continues to perform well as a reliable part of your daily life. Let's dive in and explore the best practices for keeping your iPhone in top condition, so you can focus on enjoying its many features without the frustration of unexpected issues.

Common Fixes for Wi-Fi, Bluetooth, and Apps

iPhones are highly reliable, but occasional connectivity issues or app malfunctions can still arise. Knowing how to troubleshoot these problems can save time and keep your device running smoothly. In this section, we'll cover common fixes for Wi-Fi and Bluetooth connections, as well as solutions for app-related issues. By following these steps, you'll be able to resolve many common issues yourself, without needing outside assistance.

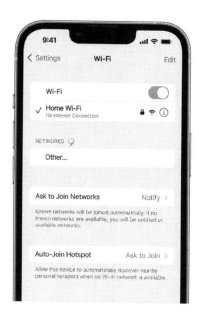

Wi-Fi connectivity is essential for internet access, app updates, and backups. If your iPhone experiences issues with connecting to Wi-Fi, try these troubleshooting steps:

- **Verify Wi-Fi Network and Password**:
  - » Ensure that your iPhone is within range of the Wi-Fi router and that you're connecting to the correct network. Verify the Wi-Fi password, especially if you've recently changed it. Go to **Settings > Wi-Fi**, select the network, and re-enter the password if prompted.

- **Forget and Reconnect to the Wi-Fi Network**:
  - » If you're experiencing slow or intermittent Wi-Fi, try forgetting the network and reconnecting. Go to **Settings > Wi-Fi**, tap the information icon (i) next to the network name, and select **Forget This Network**. Then, reconnect by selecting the network and re-entering the password.

- **Reset Network Settings**:
  - » Resetting your network settings can resolve persistent connectivity issues. Go to **Settings > General > Reset > Reset Network Settings**. This action resets all network-related settings (Wi-Fi, Bluetooth, and VPNs) but does not delete any data on your device.

- **Check Router and Internet Connection**:
  - » Sometimes the issue may be with your router or internet provider. Restart your router by unplugging it for 10 seconds and then plugging it back in. If other devices are also unable to connect, contact your internet service provider (ISP) for assistance.

- **Update iOS Software**:
  - » Software updates often include bug fixes for connectivity issues. Go to **Settings > General > Software Update** and install any available updates.

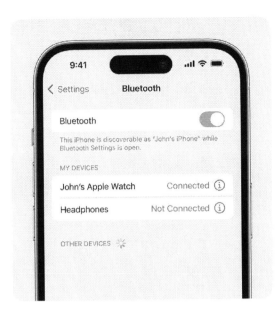

Bluetooth is essential for connecting wireless accessories like headphones, speakers, and car systems. If your iPhone has trouble connecting to Bluetooth devices, try the following steps:

- **Toggle Bluetooth Off and On**:
  - » Go to **Settings > Bluetooth** and turn Bluetooth off, wait a few seconds, then turn it back on. This simple reset can often fix minor connectivity issues.

- **Forget the Bluetooth Device and Reconnect**:
  - » If a specific Bluetooth device isn't connecting, try forgetting the device and reconnecting. In **Settings > Bluetooth**, tap the information icon (i) next to the device name, then select **Forget This Device**. Restart your Bluetooth accessory if possible, then reconnect.

- **Ensure Device Compatibility**:
  - » Some Bluetooth devices are only compatible with specific iPhone models or iOS versions. Check the manufacturer's compatibility information to ensure your device works with the iPhone 16 and iOS version you're using.

- **Reset Network Settings**:
  - » Just as with Wi-Fi, resetting your network settings can fix persistent Bluetooth issues. Go to **Settings > General > Reset > Reset Network Settings**. This will reset Bluetooth, Wi-Fi, and VPN settings, but it won't delete personal data.

- **Update Device Firmware**:
  - » Some Bluetooth devices may require firmware updates from the manufacturer to stay compatible with your iPhone. Check the device's app or website for firmware updates, as they may resolve connection issues.

- **Update iOS**:
  - » If your iPhone has an outdated iOS version, some Bluetooth devices may not function properly. Check for any available software updates by going to **Settings > General > Software Update** and install the latest iOS version.

App issues, like crashing, freezing, or slow performance, can interrupt your experience. Here's how to troubleshoot app-related problems on your iPhone:

- **Force Close the App and Reopen**:
  - » If an app is frozen or not responding, force close it and try reopening it. Swipe up from the bottom of the screen (or double-press the Home button on older models) to open the app switcher, then swipe up on the app to close it. After a few seconds, reopen the app from the Home Screen.

- **Check for App Updates**:
  - » Outdated apps can cause performance issues. Open the **App Store**, tap your profile icon, and scroll to **Available Updates**. Tap **Update All** or update individual apps that may be causing issues.

- **Restart Your iPhone**:
  - » Restarting your iPhone can resolve minor software glitches affecting app performance. To restart, press and hold the side button and either volume button, then slide to power off. Turn your iPhone back on after a few seconds by pressing the side button.

- **Clear App Cache or Data**:
  - » Some apps store cached data that can slow them down or cause crashes. In **Settings > General > iPhone Storage**, find the app and check if it offers a "Clear Cache" option (available in some apps). You can also delete and reinstall the app, which clears cached data without affecting your other data.

- **Check Storage Space**:
  - » Low storage can impact app performance and cause crashes. Go to **Settings > General > iPhone Storage** to see how much space is available. Delete unused apps, photos, or videos to free up space if needed.

- **Delete and Reinstall the App**:
  - » If an app continues to malfunction, consider deleting it and reinstalling from the App Store. This removes any corrupted files or settings associated with the app. To delete, tap and hold the app icon, select **Remove App**, and then confirm. Reinstall from the App Store once deleted.

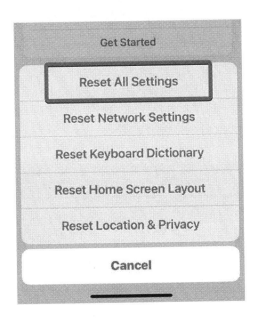

Get Started

Reset All Settings

Reset Network Settings

Reset Keyboard Dictionary

Reset Home Screen Layout

Reset Location & Privacy

Cancel

If you've tried the above methods and still experience issues with Wi-Fi, Bluetooth, or apps, here are some advanced troubleshooting steps to consider:

- **Reset All Settings**:
  - » If multiple issues persist, you may benefit from resetting all settings on your iPhone. This will not erase personal data but will reset all custom settings (e.g., Wi-Fi networks, Bluetooth devices, wallpapers). Go to **Settings > General > Reset > Reset All Settings**.

- **Restore iPhone to Factory Settings**:
  - » As a last resort, restoring your iPhone to factory settings can resolve deeper software issues. This will erase all data on your device, so make sure to back up your iPhone with iCloud or a computer first. Then go to **Settings > General > Reset > Erase All Content and Settings**. Follow the prompts to restore and then set up your iPhone as new or restore from a backup.

- **Contact Apple Support**:
  - » If all troubleshooting attempts fail, the problem may be hardware-related. Contact Apple Support or visit an Apple Store for further assistance. Apple's technicians can run diagnostics and determine if there's an underlying hardware issue that requires repair or replacement.

To keep your iPhone running smoothly, consider these tips for preventing Wi-Fi, Bluetooth, and app-related problems:

- **Regularly Restart Your iPhone**:

» Restarting your iPhone weekly can prevent minor glitches from accumulating. This clears background processes and refreshes the system, keeping your device responsive.

- **Keep Software Updated**:
  » Regularly updating iOS and your apps ensures you have the latest bug fixes and security updates. Apple frequently releases updates to improve performance and address known issues.

- **Avoid Overloading Bluetooth Connections**:
  » If you frequently use Bluetooth, avoid connecting multiple devices simultaneously, as this can cause interference. Disconnect devices that you aren't actively using to improve performance.

- **Manage Background App Activity**:
  » Some apps run in the background, using Wi-Fi, Bluetooth, and battery resources. Go to **Settings > General > Background App Refresh** and disable this feature for apps that don't require real-time updates.

- **Monitor Storage Space Regularly**:
  » Check your storage levels periodically in **Settings > General > iPhone Storage**. Keeping your iPhone storage under control reduces the risk of performance issues and app crashes.

Knowing how to troubleshoot and prevent connectivity and app issues can make using your iPhone 16 a smoother and more enjoyable experience. By following these steps, you'll be able to quickly address common problems, optimize your device's performance, and avoid disruptions. Regular maintenance, such as managing storage, updating software, and restarting periodically, will help your iPhone remain a reliable and efficient tool in your daily life. Whether it's Wi-Fi connections, Bluetooth accessories, or app-related glitches, these tips equip you to handle minor issues like a pro.

Managing Battery Life and Storage

Keeping your iPhone's battery life and storage optimized can make a big difference in daily performance, efficiency, and overall user experience. Proactive management of both helps ensure your device runs smoothly, lasts longer on a single charge, and always has space available for new apps, photos, and updates. In this section, we'll cover practical tips for extending battery life, managing app and data storage, and using built-in iPhone features to keep your device running efficiently.

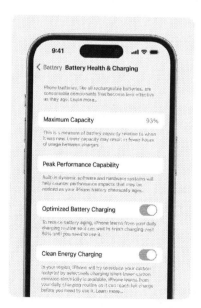

The battery in your iPhone is designed to retain optimal capacity for as long as possible, but as with any battery, its performance will degrade slightly over time. Monitoring battery health and adjusting settings accordingly can help you maintain a longer-lasting charge:

- **Check Battery Health**:

» Open **Settings > Battery > Battery Health & Charging** to view your battery's maximum capacity. This percentage shows the battery's capacity compared to when it was new. Lower capacity can mean shorter battery life between charges.

» If your battery health drops below 80%, you may consider a battery replacement to restore optimal performance.

• **Enable Optimized Battery Charging**:

» Optimized Battery Charging helps slow down battery aging by learning your charging routine and reducing the time your battery spends fully charged. Enable this feature in **Settings > Battery > Battery Health & Charging**. Your iPhone will hold the charge at 80% during long charges (like overnight) and complete the final 20% close to the time you typically start using it.

• **Low Power Mode**:

» Low Power Mode reduces battery drain by pausing certain background tasks, decreasing screen brightness, and limiting animations. To activate, go to **Settings > Battery** or enable it from the Control Center. Use Low Power Mode when your battery is low or when you know you won't be able to charge for a while.

Adjusting a few settings can have a significant impact on your iPhone's battery life. Here are some tips to reduce power consumption without sacrificing functionality:

• **Adjust Screen Brightness and Enable Auto-Brightness**:

» The screen is one of the biggest battery drains on your device. Lowering the brightness manually or enabling Auto-Brightness, which adjusts brightness based on ambient light, can extend battery life. Go to **Settings > Display & Brightness** and toggle **Auto-Brightness**.

• **Manage Background App Refresh**:

» Apps that update in the background use up battery power. Limit this feature by going to **Settings > General > Background App Refresh** and selecting **Off** or **Wi-Fi only**. Alternatively, turn it off for specific apps that don't need constant updating.

• **Disable Location Services for Unnecessary Apps**:

» Location Services uses GPS, which can quickly drain your battery. Go to **Settings > Privacy > Location Services** and turn off Location Services for apps that don't need location tracking or change their setting to **While Using the App**.

• **Turn Off Push Notifications for Non-Essential Apps**:

» Each push notification wakes your iPhone and uses battery power. Disable notifications for apps that don't require real-time alerts by going to **Settings > Notifications** and turning off **Allow Notifications** for individual apps.

• **Use Dark Mode**:

» Dark Mode can save battery life on iPhones with OLED screens (such as the iPhone 16) by reducing the amount of light emitted. Go to **Settings > Display & Brightness** and select **Dark** mode. You can also set Dark Mode to activate automatically in low-light conditions or based on a schedule.

Keeping your iPhone's storage clear is essential for smooth performance and avoiding slowdowns. Here are strategies for managing and optimizing storage:

- **View and Manage Storage Usage**:
  - » Go to **Settings > General > iPhone Storage** to view a breakdown of storage usage. You'll see how much space each app takes up, as well as options to delete apps or files directly. Regularly check this screen to see which apps or files are using the most space.

- **Enable iCloud Photo Library**:
  - » Photos and videos are major storage users. Enabling **iCloud Photos** can help free up local storage by storing original, full-resolution images in iCloud and keeping optimized versions on your device. To enable, go to **Settings > Photos** and toggle on **iCloud Photos**.

- **Offload Unused Apps**:
  - » Offloading removes apps you don't frequently use but keeps their data saved, so you can easily reinstall them later without losing data. Go to **Settings > General > iPhone Storage**, scroll to **Offload Unused Apps**, and select **Enable**. You can also offload individual apps in the iPhone Storage menu.

- **Clear Cache and Unnecessary Data**:
  - » Some apps, such as social media and streaming apps, accumulate cache files that take up storage. While not all apps have a built-in option to clear cache, deleting and reinstalling these apps will remove cached data, freeing up space without losing core data.

- **Delete Old Messages and Attachments**:
  - » Messages, especially those with photos and videos, can take up significant space. Go to **Settings > Messages** and set **Message History** to delete messages after 30 days or 1 year, depending on your preference.

iCloud can be a great tool for expanding your storage capacity without overloading your iPhone. Here are ways to use iCloud and other external options:

- **Upgrade iCloud Storage**:
  - » If you need more storage, consider upgrading your iCloud plan. iCloud offers several affordable plans with additional storage, making it easy to back up your photos, files, and app data. Go to **Settings > [Your Name] > iCloud > Manage Storage** to see available options.

- **iCloud Drive for Document Storage**:
  - » iCloud Drive allows you to store documents and files in the cloud, freeing up space on your iPhone. Files saved in iCloud Drive are accessible on all Apple devices, so you can offload larger files and access them anytime.

- **Use External Storage Devices**:
  - » You can also connect external storage devices (e.g., USB drives with a Lightning connector or compatible SSDs) to your iPhone using adapters. Use the **Files** app to transfer larger files to these external devices when needed.

Performing regular maintenance on your iPhone can help maintain battery life and storage space over the long term:

- **Restart Your iPhone Periodically**:

» Restarting your iPhone weekly can help clear out temporary files and reset background processes, which can improve performance and battery life.

- **Update Apps and iOS Regularly**:

  » App and system updates often include performance improvements and bug fixes that can positively affect battery life. Go to the **App Store** to check for app updates, and check **Settings > General > Software Update** for iOS updates.

- **Clear Safari Cache and Data**:

  » If you frequently use Safari, its cache may accumulate over time. Clear Safari data by going to **Settings > Safari > Clear History and Website Data**. This can help free up space and improve browsing speed.

- **Limit Background Processes**:

  » If your iPhone is running slow or experiencing battery drain, check background processes. In **Settings > General > Background App Refresh**, disable background refresh for apps that don't need it.

- **Battery Replacement as Needed**:

  » If your iPhone's battery health has significantly declined, consider getting a battery replacement. Apple provides battery replacement services that can restore performance, especially if your device's battery capacity is below 80%.

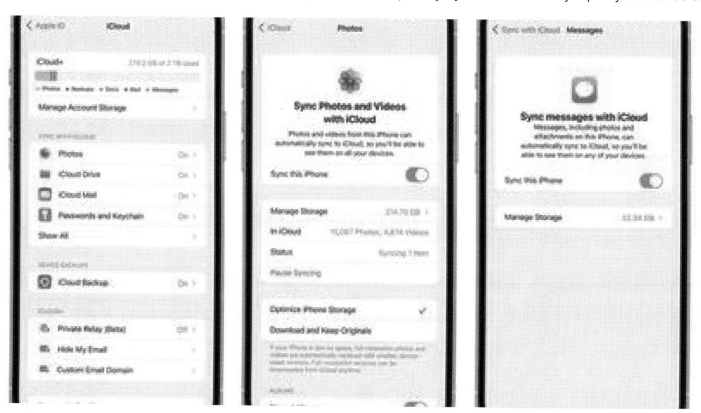

Your iPhone 16 provides alerts and notifications to help you manage battery life and storage. Pay attention to these warnings to keep your device optimized:

- **Battery Usage Alerts**:

  » The Health app will notify you if your battery usage is higher than usual. These notifications can help identify apps or features that are draining your battery, allowing you to adjust settings as needed.

- **Storage Warnings**:

  » When your storage is nearly full, your iPhone will notify you with suggestions for freeing up space, such as offloading unused apps or deleting large files. Follow these prompts to keep your device performing well.

- **Reviewing Battery and Storage Trends**:

» Regularly checking battery and storage trends in **Settings > Battery** and **Settings > General > iPhone Storage** can help you maintain both resources efficiently.

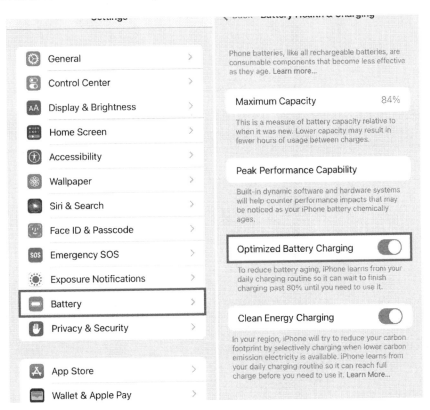

Extending your battery's lifespan is possible with a few simple habits:

- **Avoid Extreme Temperatures**:
  » High or low temperatures can affect battery life. Try to keep your iPhone between 32° and 95° Fahrenheit to avoid stress on the battery.

- **Avoid Overcharging**:
  » Charging your iPhone overnight occasionally is fine, but avoid keeping it on the charger for extended periods once it reaches 100%, as this can shorten the battery lifespan. **Optimized Battery Charging** can help manage this automatically.

- **Limit Fast Charging for Routine Charges**:
  » Fast charging is convenient, but it generates more heat, which can impact battery health over time. Use a standard charger when possible, especially for overnight charging.

Properly managing battery life and storage on your iPhone 16 can make a world of difference in performance and longevity. By making small adjustments to settings, keeping storage optimized, using iCloud, and following best practices for battery health, you can keep your device running smoothly and reliably for years. Following these steps ensures your iPhone is ready to support your daily needs without unexpected slowdowns or low battery warnings.

Backing Up and Restoring Data with iCloud

Backing up your iPhone with iCloud is an essential part of protecting your data. Whether you're upgrading to a new device, troubleshooting an issue, or ensuring your information is safe in case of loss or damage, iCloud's backup and restore features provide a reliable and seamless way to keep your data secure and accessible. In this section, we'll cover how to set up automatic iCloud backups, manage backup storage, restore data from a backup, and use additional iCloud features to keep your important files and settings synchronized across devices.

iCloud Backup automatically saves a copy of most data on your iPhone, including app data, device settings, messages, photos, and videos. Here's a breakdown of what iCloud backup covers and what it excludes:

- **Included in iCloud Backup**:

  » **App Data**: Data from apps installed on your iPhone.
  » **Device Settings**: Configuration settings, including Wi-Fi networks, custom preferences, and more.
  » **Messages**: iMessages, SMS, and MMS messages.
  » **Photos and Videos**: If you use iCloud Photos, your photos and videos are stored in iCloud and can be restored easily.
  » **Visual Voicemail**: Any saved voicemail messages.
  » **Health Data and HomeKit Configurations**: Important for users who track fitness or use smart home devices.

- **Excluded from iCloud Backup**:

  » **Data already stored in iCloud**: For example, contacts, calendars, notes, and reminders are not included in backups because they are synced through iCloud services independently.
  » **Music, Movies, and Podcasts**: Items purchased from iTunes or other media files are not backed up because they can be re-downloaded.

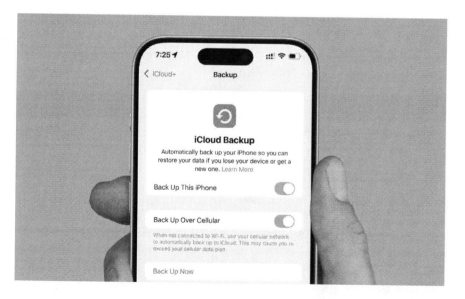

Automatic iCloud backups are the most convenient way to ensure your data is backed up regularly. Here's how to set it up:

- **Step 1: Connect to Wi-Fi**:

» iCloud backups require a stable Wi-Fi connection, as cellular data does not support this feature due to data usage constraints. Make sure you are connected to a Wi-Fi network before starting.

Step 2: Enable iCloud Backup:

» Go to **Settings > [Your Name] > iCloud > iCloud Backup** and toggle on **iCloud Backup**. With this feature enabled, your iPhone will automatically back up data to iCloud once it's connected to Wi-Fi, plugged in, and locked.

Step 3: Perform a Manual Backup:

» To create an immediate backup, tap **Back Up Now** in the iCloud Backup settings. This is helpful if you want to ensure the latest version of your data is saved, especially before major changes like an iOS update or a device reset.

Schedule and Conditions for Automatic Backups:

» iCloud automatically performs backups daily, as long as your device is connected to Wi-Fi, plugged in to charge, and locked. Regular automatic backups ensure that your data is up-to-date with minimal effort on your part.

Apple offers 5GB of free iCloud storage, but additional storage is often necessary, especially if you have a large photo library or multiple devices. Here's how to manage iCloud storage and free up space as needed:

Viewing iCloud Storage Usage:

» Go to **Settings > [Your Name] > iCloud > Manage Storage** to see a breakdown of what's using your iCloud storage. This menu provides a detailed list of backups, apps, and files stored in iCloud.

Upgrading iCloud Storage:

» If you need more space, consider upgrading your storage plan. Apple offers plans from 50GB to 2TB, starting at a reasonable monthly fee. To upgrade, go to **Settings > [Your Name] > iCloud > Manage Storage > Change Storage Plan**.

Removing Unnecessary Backups:

» If you have backups from older devices you no longer use, consider deleting them to free up space. In the Manage Storage menu, select **Backups**, then tap the backup you wish to delete and select **Delete Backup**.

Optimizing Photo and Video Storage:

» If photos and videos are taking up too much space, enable **iCloud Photos** and select **Optimize iPhone Storage** in **Settings > Photos**. This stores full-resolution photos and videos in iCloud while keeping smaller versions on your device.

Restoring your data from an iCloud backup is useful if you're setting up a new iPhone or recovering data after a reset. Follow these steps to restore data:

- **Step 1: Reset Your Device** (If Already Set Up):
  - » To restore from an iCloud backup, you need to erase the current data on your iPhone. Go to **Settings > General > Reset > Erase All Content and Settings** and confirm. This will restart your iPhone and take you to the setup screen.

- **Step 2: Set Up Your iPhone**:
  - » Follow the setup prompts until you reach the **Apps & Data** screen. Here, select **Restore from iCloud Backup** and sign in to iCloud with your Apple ID.

- **Step 3: Choose a Backup**:
  - » You'll see a list of available backups. Choose the most recent one or the one with the data you want to restore. The restoration process will begin, and your data, including settings, app data, and messages, will be downloaded to your device.

- **Completing the Restore Process**:
  - » The time required to restore depends on the size of the backup and your Wi-Fi connection speed. Once the restore is complete, your iPhone will restart with all the backed-up data. Note that large files like photos and videos may take extra time to finish downloading in the background.

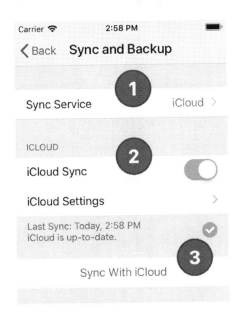

Beyond backups, iCloud also offers data synchronization across Apple devices, keeping your information updated and accessible on your iPhone, iPad, Mac, and more:

- **Syncing Contacts, Calendars, and Notes**:
  » iCloud automatically syncs contacts, calendar events, notes, reminders, and other data across all your Apple devices. Go to **Settings > [Your Name] > iCloud** and toggle on services you want to sync. This continuous sync keeps your information updated everywhere.

- **Using iCloud Drive for Files**:
  » iCloud Drive allows you to store documents and files that you can access on any Apple device or through iCloud. com. Store files here that don't need to be backed up individually and access them on demand.

- **Accessing iCloud Files on Non-Apple Devices**:
  » You can access files, photos, and documents stored in iCloud from any browser by visiting **iCloud.com** and logging in with your Apple ID. This feature is useful for accessing your data when you're on a non-Apple device.

Consistency with backups is essential for ensuring that you never lose data. Here are some tips to maintain a reliable backup routine:

- **Perform Manual Backups Before Major Changes**:

» Perform a manual backup before upgrading iOS, installing significant updates, or making big changes to your iPhone This ensures that your data is secure and recoverable.

- **Check Backup Status Regularly**:
  » Periodically check the status of your iCloud backup to make sure it's running smoothly. In **Settings > [Your Name] > iCloud > iCloud Backup**, you'll see the date and time of your last successful backup. If backups aren't happening automatically, troubleshoot any connectivity or storage issues.

- **Consider Creating Local Backups on a Computer**:
  » In addition to iCloud backups, you can create local backups using a computer and iTunes (or Finder on macOS Catalina and later). This gives you a secondary backup option that's stored independently from iCloud.

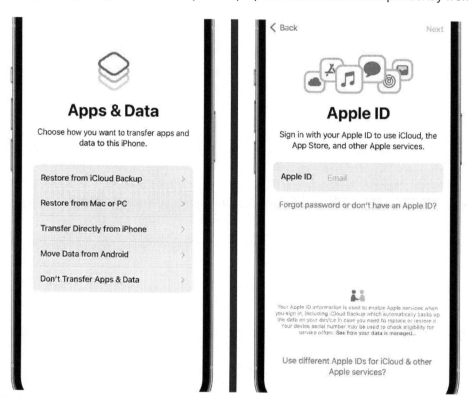

Sometimes, you may only need to recover specific types of data rather than restoring a full backup:

- **Photos and Videos**:
  » If you have **iCloud Photos** enabled, your photos and videos are continuously synced and stored in iCloud, allowing you to recover them independently of a full backup. Go to **Photos** and log in with your Apple ID to re-download them if needed.

- **Messages and Contacts**:
  » Contacts, messages, and other iCloud-synced items are automatically restored when you log back into your Apple ID on a new or reset device.

- **Files from iCloud Drive**:
  » Any documents saved in **iCloud Drive** are accessible by logging into iCloud on any Apple device or through iCloud. com. This feature lets you retrieve documents without restoring the full device backup.

iCloud's backup and restore features make it easy to safeguard your iPhone's data and seamlessly recover it when needed. By setting up automatic backups, managing iCloud storage, and knowing how to restore data from iCloud, you can confidently protect your information and access it across all your Apple devices. Whether you're switching to a new iPhone, troubleshooting, or ensuring your data is secure, regular backups are an essential practice to keep your digital life safe and accessible.

CONCLUSION

As we conclude this guide to mastering the iPhone 16, let's take a moment to reflect on the journey we've covered—from initial setup to advanced troubleshooting and maintenance. This guide has been designed to empower users of all experience levels, particularly those new to smartphones or those looking to deepen their understanding of the iPhone 16's capabilities. From configuring the device to align with your personal preferences to troubleshooting common issues, each chapter has provided practical steps, tips, and best practices for navigating the iPhone 16 with confidence.

Your iPhone 16 is more than a communication device; it's a comprehensive tool that can support you in staying connected, maintaining your health, exploring creative outlets, managing finances, and safeguarding your data. Equipped with powerful features like Apple Pay, iCloud, Health, and robust accessibility options, the iPhone is designed to integrate seamlessly into every aspect of daily life. Whether you want to FaceTime with family, track your health metrics, or use Apple Pay at the grocery store, each of these tools is at your fingertips. The possibilities are endless, and the more familiar you become with these features, the more value you'll unlock from your device.

Your Path to a Personalized Experience

One of the iPhone 16's greatest strengths lies in its customization options, allowing each user to tailor the device to meet their unique needs. In earlier chapters, we explored how to adjust display brightness, text size, and accessibility settings, ensuring that you can use the iPhone comfortably, regardless of any vision or hearing limitations. Customization doesn't stop at accessibility; it extends to everything from organizing your apps and adjusting notification settings to setting up a digital wallet that simplifies financial transactions.

For seniors and beginners, this customization is especially valuable, as it transforms the iPhone from a standard smartphone into a highly personalized and intuitive tool. When you can adjust the iPhone to cater to your individual preferences, you're not just using a device—you're creating a personalized digital environment that feels accessible, familiar, and enjoyable.

Staying Connected with Family and Friends

A major motivation for many iPhone users, especially seniors, is the desire to stay in touch with loved ones. The iPhone 16 makes this effortless through features like Messages, FaceTime, and shared photo albums, which provide seamless ways to connect with family and friends. With FaceTime, you can share special moments and catch up with distant relatives, while shared photo albums allow you to stay updated on the latest family events. The iPhone also supports a variety of social media and messaging apps, making it easy to keep up with family members who use different platforms.

Additionally, the Messages app offers features like sending multimedia messages, using emojis, and even sharing location—making communication not only functional but also fun. Staying connected is vital to well-being, and the iPhone provides the tools to make that connection easy, whether you're a few miles or a few thousand miles apart.

Health and Safety at the Forefront

Another invaluable benefit of the iPhone 16 is its health and safety features, which are designed with accessibility, privacy, and usability in mind. The Health app is a powerful resource for tracking fitness, sleep, and mindfulness, enabling users to take a proactive approach to wellness. Setting up Medical ID and emergency contacts ensures that first responders have access to critical information in case of an emergency—a simple feature that can make a significant difference in urgent situations.

Safety is also a priority in the iPhone's online environment. With privacy-focused settings and regular security updates, the iPhone keeps your personal information protected. The device's built-in security tools, like Face ID, Touch ID, and App Permissions, safeguard against unauthorized access and minimize the risk of privacy breaches. By staying familiar with these features, you can use your iPhone with the confidence that your personal information is well-protected.

A Practical Guide for Troubleshooting and Maintenance

Every technology comes with its occasional challenges, and the iPhone is no exception. However, one of the benefits of Apple's design philosophy is its emphasis on ease of use and customer support. In this guide, we've covered practical troubleshooting tips for common issues, from Wi-Fi and Bluetooth connections to app crashes and storage management. Knowing how to reset network settings, manage background activity, and optimize battery life gives you the power to resolve most minor issues on your own.

The maintenance practices outlined in this guide—such as regular backups, storage management, and software updates— are equally essential for keeping your device running smoothly over time. By taking these small but effective steps, you can maximize your iPhone's lifespan and avoid disruptions in your daily routine. When more complex issues arise, Apple's comprehensive support resources are readily available, including online documentation, customer service, and in-store assistance from Apple's Genius Bar. The more proactive you are about maintaining your device, the more reliable it will be.

Embracing a Digital Lifestyle with Confidence

For many beginners and seniors, using a smartphone can initially feel daunting. But as you've explored the features of the iPhone 16 throughout this guide, hopefully, any initial apprehension has been replaced with a sense of confidence and curiosity. The iPhone is designed to be user-friendly, and with a little practice, navigating its features can become second nature. By building familiarity with everyday tasks—such as taking photos, using Maps, or managing contacts—you're not only enhancing your digital skills but also expanding the ways you can interact with the world around you.

Embracing technology at any age is an empowering experience, and learning to use the iPhone 16 effectively can open up new possibilities for communication, creativity, learning, and enjoyment. Whether it's sending your first text, setting up a personalized home screen, or making a video call, each new skill is a step toward greater independence and engagement in today's digital world.

Continuous Learning and Exploration

Technology is constantly evolving, and so are the features on your iPhone. Apple regularly releases updates that introduce new capabilities, improve performance, and enhance security. By keeping your iPhone updated and exploring new features as they become available, you can continue to make the most of your device. Consider revisiting certain features or exploring new apps periodically, as they can add even more value to your iPhone experience.

Furthermore, online communities, tutorials, and Apple's own resources provide a wealth of information for users interested in deepening their knowledge. You don't have to be an expert to enjoy the benefits of your iPhone; just a willingness to explore and learn can lead to unexpected discoveries. Technology is a lifelong journey, and with the support of resources and communities, there's always something new to learn.

Looking Ahead: The Future with Your iPhone

The iPhone 16 is a powerful tool that has the potential to make daily tasks easier, help you connect with the people you care about, and open doors to new experiences. As technology continues to progress, so will the opportunities for using your iPhone in ways that are meaningful and beneficial to you. Whether it's discovering new apps, finding innovative ways to stay organized, or exploring the latest health and wellness features, the iPhone is designed to evolve with your needs and adapt to new possibilities.

As you grow more familiar with its capabilities, you may find that the iPhone becomes an integral part of your day-to-day life. It's more than just a device; it's a companion that can support you in ways that matter most, from staying in touch with loved ones to organizing daily tasks and preserving your memories. The iPhone is truly a device built with the user in mind, continually evolving to serve your unique needs and preferences.

Final Thoughts

As we wrap up this guide, remember that the iPhone 16 is a versatile and intuitive device that can be as simple or as sophisticated as you need it to be. For beginners and seniors, it offers ease of use, reliability, and a wide range of features designed to make life easier and more enjoyable. Embracing the iPhone is not just about keeping up with technology; it's about enhancing your lifestyle in meaningful ways, whether that's through more frequent communication with family, engaging in new hobbies, or staying active and healthy.

Thank you for taking this journey through the iPhone 16 guide. By equipping yourself with knowledge and exploring each feature at your own pace, you've gained the tools to use this device confidently and effectively. Your iPhone is now ready to support you in new adventures, day-to-day tasks, and lifelong learning. Remember, technology is here to enhance, not overwhelm—and with this guide, you're more than ready to make the most of your iPhone experience. Enjoy the endless possibilities and the journey ahead with your iPhone 16!

GET YOUR EXCLUSIVE BONUS

Scan the QR-CODE below and get your exclusive bonus

iPhone 16 Video Tutorial

iPhone 16 Pro Video Tutorial

Made in the USA
Columbia, SC
23 March 2025

55265834R00111